TUSKEGEE

PHOTOGRAPH BY CHICKERING.

Booker T. Washington.

TUSKEGEE
Its Story and Its Work

BY

MAX BENNETT THRASHER

With an Introduction by
BOOKER T. WASHINGTON

The Black Heritage Library Collection

BOOKS FOR LIBRARIES PRESS
FREEPORT, NEW YORK
1971

First Published 1900
Reprinted 1971

Reprinted from a copy in the
Fisk University Library Negro Collection

INTERNATIONAL STANDARD BOOK NUMBER:
0-8369-8833-7

LIBRARY OF CONGRESS CATALOG CARD NUMBER:
77-161274

PRINTED IN THE UNITED STATES OF AMERICA

*To the young men and women
graduates and students of Tuskegee*

PREFACE.

During the last five years I have made several visits to Alabama to study the methods and work of Tuskegee Normal and Industrial Institute for colored students, and to attend the annual sessions of the Tuskegee Negro Conference, an outgrowth of the Institute. I have visited many graduates and students of the school at work and in their homes, over a territory extending from West Virginia to Louisiana. In doing this work I have had opportunities to hear Mr. Booker T. Washington, the principal of the Institute, address many audiences of people of both races, North and South, and under widely varying conditions.

As a result of my observations during this time I have brought together here a more comprehensive account of the Institute, and of Mr. Washington's connection with it, than has been possible in any of several newspaper and magazine articles which I have written. To the publications in which these articles have appeared from time to time I wish to make grateful acknowledgment for any material from them which I may have included in this volume.

I also wish to acknowledge my obligations to Mr. Wm. H. Baldwin, Jr., of New York, who has read the manuscript, and to whose advice and suggestions I am greatly indebted.

MAX BENNETT THRASHER.

Boston, Mass.

vii

CONTENTS.

———◆◇◆———

CONTENTS.

CONTENTS.

CONTENTS.

LIST OF ILLUSTRATIONS.

LIST OF ILLUSTRATIONS.

INTRODUCTION.

Mr. Max Bennett Thrasher, the author of this little volume, has exceptional fitness for the work that he has done. For a number of years he has been closely acquainted with the Tuskegee Normal and Industrial Institute and its work. He has made many visits to the institution and studied its work closely upon the grounds. Besides being a newspaper writer of experience and talent, he has taken the precaution to travel carefully through many of our Southern States, and in speaking of the work of the graduates from Tuskegee he tells that which he has actually seen and examined into. Few persons have had a better opportunity to judge of the value of Tuskegee's graduates than Mr. Thrasher. He has not only studied carefully the influence of our students in building up the colored people in the various communities where they are laboring as teachers, farmers, mechanics, etc., but what is equally important, he has noted carefully the influence of these men and women in bringing about a better sentiment between the races. Any one who wants to get first hand information in regard to the work of such institutions as Tuskegee and the power exerted through the graduates can find few better sources of information than is contained in Mr. Thrasher's book, and I bespeak for it a careful reading by all who are interested in our great Southern problem, which, to be more precise, is not a Southern problem, but a national problem in which North and South should be equally interested.

Mr. Thrasher's book bears out the statement which I have often made, that the wisest and most economic policy to pursue in lifting up the black race in the South is to equip well certain large central institutions which can send out a constant stream of unselfish, wise, Christian leaders who are well fortified with academic and industrial training, and who will settle in small communities and show the people themselves how to improve their schools and industrial and religious condition. This was the policy which the late General S. C. Armstrong, the Principal of the Hampton Institute, so wisely outlined years ago, and the one which is being so carefully and successfully followed by his successor, Dr. H. B. Frissell. Every black man who is so trained that he can do something better than somebody else, can do a common thing in an uncommon manner, can make himself indispensable in the community where he lives, not only helps our own race but secures at the same time the respect, confidence, and coöperation of the Southern white people in the community where he lives. All who are interested in the proper solution of the problem in the South should feel deeply grateful to Mr. Thrasher for the task which he has undertaken and performed so well.

BOOKER T. WASHINGTON.

Tuskegee Normal and Industrial Institute, Tuskegee, Alabama, September 1, 1900.

TUSKEGEE
Its Story and Its Work

CHAPTER I.

NOT long after the Civil War had closed, a Negro boy, who had been born a slave and freed by the war, was learning to read in the spare minutes of his work as general chore-boy about a West Virginia farmhouse. Sometimes, late at night, after he had gone to bed in that one of the houses of "the quarters" in which he slept, the boy would tell himself that some day, when he had grown to be a man, he meant to found a school for Negro boys and girls which should grow to be so great and famous that even the President of the United States would come to visit it.

The dream in the outbuilding among the West Virginia mountains has come true. The boy was Booker Washington. The school which he founded at Tuskegee, Alabama, he has developed until now more than a thousand young Negro men and women are taught there every year to make their lives count for the most possible for themselves and for their race. In the autumn of the year 1898, when President McKinley, accompanied by his cabinet and several prominent generals of the United States Army, made a journey through the South, they spent one entire day visiting Tuskegee Normal and Industrial Institute. At that time the President, speaking in public, said: —

" To speak of Tuskegee without paying special tribute to Booker T. Washington's genius and perseverance, would be impossible. The inception of this noble enterprise was his, and he deserves high credit for it. His was the enthusiasm and enterprise which made its steady progress possible, and established in the institute its present high standard of accomplishment. He has won a worthy reputation as one of the great leaders of his race, widely known and much respected at home and abroad as an accomplished educator, a great orator, and a true philanthropist."

President McKinley has said that it would be impossible to speak of Tuskegee without paying tribute to Booker T. Washington. It would be equally impossible to write fully and comprehensively of Tuskegee without giving some account of Mr. Washington's life before he founded the school. The circumstances under which his boyhood and youth were passed, and the obstacles with which he had to contend, were very generally the common lot of the people of his race, to aid whom Tuskegee was established. His own experiences enabled him to understand the needs of others and roused in him an ambition to try and satisfy those needs.

Booker Washington was born a slave on a plantation near Hale's Ford, in Virginia. He does not know just when, for the coming into the world of one more black baby on a slave plantation was a matter of so little account that

TINSHOP FLOAT IN PROCESSION IN HONOR OF PRESIDENT MCKINLEY'S VISIT.

frequently no record of the event was kept
which would accurately fix the date.   Probably
Mr. Washington was born in 1857 or 1858,
though, as one of his earliest recollections is of
hearing the Negroes talk in whispers in their
cabins at night about a war which was being
fought around them.   As he has a quite natural
desire to have a birthday, Mr. Washington usually selects Easter Sunday for that celebration.

The home into which the black baby came
was of the humblest — a windowless, one-room
log cabin, with the earth itself for the floor. Not
long ago I heard Mr. Washington say, " My first
memory of life is that of a one-room log cabin
with a dirt floor that had a hole in the center
which served as a winter home for sweet potatoes.
Wrapped in a few rags I spent my nights on this
dirt floor, and clad in a single garment I often
spent my days about the plantation."

Another memory of those early days I heard
him recall to a great audience of his own people
in a southern city.   He had been speaking of
Lincoln, and said, " My first acquaintance with
our hero was this : Night after night, before the
dawn of day, on an old slave plantation in Virginia, I recall the form of my sainted mother,
bending over a bundle of rags that enveloped my
body, on a dirt floor, breathing a fervent prayer
to Heaven that ' Massa Lincoln ' might succeed,
and that some day she and I might be free."

No one who has seen much of Booker Washington can fail to have been impressed by his

affection for his mother while she lived, and his devotion to her memory. I think her influence is often made manifest through him, even now, although, perhaps, he may not be conscious of the fact at the time. I have frequently heard him tell his own students, or those of other schools, " The learning which you acquire is of no use to you unless it makes you better able to live. The knowledge which you acquire from books is of use only as you apply it. Young man, use your knowledge of geometry to help your father lay out his cotton rows, your knowledge of chemistry to show him how to raise better crops. Young woman, use your knowledge of chemistry to help your mother in her cooking and washing, your skill in embroidery to assist her in the family mending. When you go home from school to-night, or at the end of the term, put on your overalls, young man, and say, ' Father, you have borne the heat of the day in putting in the crops ; go you now and sit in the shade and rest, while I hoe the crop or do the milking.' Young woman, when you go home, tie on an apron and say, ' Now, mother, you must be tired ; sit down and rest while I do the washing or ironing, and get supper.' And, mark my words, the heart of that father and that mother will leap for joy, and they will say, ' Nothing of all the hard work that we have done that our children may go to school has been too hard, for they appreciate our sacrifices and are making the most of their opportunities."

CHAPTER II.

ONE day a Negro woman running through "the quarters" thrust her head inside the door of Washington's mother's cabin, and shouted, "Praise Gawd! We 's all done sent for to come up to de big house." A little later, to all the slaves, men, women and children, gathered in the yard in front of the house, some one standing on the verandah read a paper. Washington was too young to comprehend the words, or to understand why the men and women around him should jump up and down and shout, "Glory Hallelujah! Praise de Lawd!" But his mother, bending down to where he was clinging to her dress, whispered to him that now they were free.

When the coming of freedom made it possible for them to seek a new home, Mr. Washington's mother and her family crossed the mountains into the western part of West Virginia, where work which would pay money wages could be had, in the coal mines and salt furnaces of that region. Their destination was Malden, a little village on the banks of the Kanawha river, five miles above the city of Charleston. Here the children worked to help support the home. Booker found employment in a coal mine as a "miner's helper," at fifty cents a day, or drove one of the mules used to drag the coal-laden

cars out of the mine. At other times he worked
at one of the salt furnaces, packing the dry salt
into barrels, or shoveling the salt off from the
platform above the tanks of boiling brine, where
it had been piled to drain, — always a dangerous
work, — since a misstep meant almost certain
death.

In the summer of 1899 I visited Charleston,
West Virginia, with Mr. Washington, and we
spent one whole day going about among these
scenes of his boyhood. The coal mine where he
worked had been "blown out," that is, abandoned, some years before; but an increased demand for coal had attracted attention to it again,
and when we were there the gallery was being
cleared of debris preparatory to being opened for
work. Of the salt furnace at which Mr. Washington worked nothing remained but the ruins
of a huge stone chimney rising from a cornfield.

During the first year that the family lived in
West Virginia, a young man by the name of
William Davis, who had recently been mustered
out of service as a member of the Ohio troops in
the late war, came to Malden and contracted to
teach a subscription school there for colored
children. Washington's mother was one of the
subscribers, and the boy Booker began his education under this man, from whom he learned
his letters. Mr. Davis is now living in Charleston, where I went to see him. He told me that
Washington was a slow scholar in arithmetic, but
quick to learn to read, and always an easy and

ready speaker. The account which Mr. Washington gives of how he first came to want to go to school may give a hint as to the reason for his fondness for reading. "One day," he says, " I happened to see a group of colored men gathered around another man who knew how to read, and who was reading aloud to them from a piece of newspaper. The man's hearers gazed at him with mouths and eyes wide open with admiration, as he slowly spelled out the words. He was little less than a god to them. I resolved at once that I would acquire an art which could give a man such a power over his fellows, and from that day I watched for a chance to go to school."

When Washington was about twelve years old he was hired by a white woman, Mrs. Viola Ruffner, who lived in Malden, to work for her as a general chore-boy in and about the house. Mrs. Ruffner was a northern woman, a native of Vermont, who had married and settled in West Virginia. She was a woman of remarkable force of character and great kindness of heart. When she came to understand the ambitions of her new kitchen boy, she took pains to help him in many ways. Much of this time he remained a pupil in the village night school, but Mrs. Ruffner helped him greatly with his studies. Not long before I went to Malden I had the pleasure of visiting Mrs. Ruffner at her home. She was then living in Charleston, South Carolina, with her son, Major E. H. Ruffner. From her I heard many personal reminiscences of those early years of the colored boy, in whose successful later life she has always taken a warm interest. " Booker was always a good boy," she said, " and never wasted his time, as so many servants did. If he had a few minutes of spare time he would sit down in a corner of the kitchen and study his reading lesson ; and more than once I have seen a light between twelve and one o'clock in the out-building where he slept, and have gone there to make him stop studying, put out his light and go to bed, because I knew he had to.get up early the next morning to go to peddle vegetables at the furnaces down the river. He was never satisfied unless he was doing something to help himself ' get on in the world.' I remember he left me two or three times for other work which seemed to offer greater opportunities, — once going to work on one of the river steamboats, — but he always came back, until he left me to go to Hampton."

While Mr. Washington was spending a few weeks in Europe, for a rest, in the summer of 1899, he received an invitation from the governor of West Virginia, the city government of Charleston, and a great number of prominent citizens of both races, to visit Charleston on his return to this country, that there might be given him there a series of receptions which would testify the respect felt by the citizens of his old home for him and for his work. This invitation was accepted, and it was at this time, in August and September, 1899, that I visited West Virginia with Mr. Washington. At that time, speaking in public to a great audience of both races assembled in the opera house in Charleston, he paid this tribute to Mrs. Ruffner : —

" Not far from here, in the family of a noble white woman whom most of you know, I received a training in the matters of thoroughness, cleanliness, promptness and honesty, which, I confess to you, in a large measure, enables me to do the work for which I am given credit. As I look over my life I feel that the training which I received in the family of Mrs. Viola Ruffner was a most valuable part of my education."

While we were at Malden we visited the Ruffner house, which is still in the possession of the family, and I secured several pictures of Mr. Washington amid scenes which were associated with his early life there. The Kanawha valley, at Malden, is little more than a mountain gorge. The Ruffner house stands facing the river, across which the trains of the Chesapeake and Ohio railroad leave black smoke wreaths against the sky. The house is so close to the bank that one standing at the garden fence can toss a stone into the water. While we stood there looking at the hills which shut the valley in so closely, Mr. Washington said : " When I was a boy these mountains looked so high to me, I remember I used to wonder what was behind them, and wish I could climb to the tops and see." I thought to myself at the time that few persons have had their wishes more fully gratified.

The first house in which Mr. Washington's mother lived when they came to Malden is gone entirely. This was a log house, and we could find no trace of it, except a few bricks of the chimney buried in a forest of weeds. The house in which the family lived when Booker started for Hampton is still standing, in good repair. We also visited " Father Rice, " the grizzled old Negro preacher who was Washington's first Sunday-school teacher. He has lived in Malden all these years. He was delighted to see his former pupil, of whose fame now he had heard rumors, and gladly consented to stand with him in front of the parsonage that they might be photographed together. I asked him how Mr. Washington behaved in Sunday-school, when he was a boy, and he said, " Ah hain't nuffin to say agi'n' him. He was allus a good boy. "

It was while the boy, Booker, was at work for Mrs. Ruffner that he heard of General Armstrong's school at Hampton as a place where black boys would be taught, and at the same time be allowed to work to pay their expenses. This was just the chance "to get on in the world, " for which Mrs. Ruffner told me he was always looking. He resolved at once to go to Hampton, although he had almost no money, and did not even know definitely where Hampton was. His mother and brother added what little money they could spare to his savings, and bidding them and Mrs. Ruffner good-by, he set out. Even with what had been given him, the boy had money enough to pay his stage fare and car fare for only a portion of the journey over the mountains to the sea. He rode when he could, and walked the rest of the way, working here and there for food and lodging, and frequently sleeping in barns or by the roadside. In this way, inquiring the route as he went, he reached the city of Richmond, Virginia, too late one night to find work, and absolutely out of money with which to secure a lodging.

I once heard him tell the story of that night to an audience in Columbia, South Carolina. "It was nearly midnight," he said. "I had walked about for a long time, not knowing what to do, and hoping that some opportunity for work might present itself. Finally I found myself on a stretch of plank sidewalk near the river. I saw a good, dry place under the sidewalk. There was no one in sight. I crawled in, curled up and went to sleep. When I woke it was morning, and I found myself near a vessel which had just come in and which had a cargo to be unloaded. I secured a chance to help at this, and as the work lasted for several days, I came back to the same place under the sidewalk to sleep each night, that I might save the money which otherwise it would have cost me for lodging. In this way, I earned enough money to pay my fare the rest of the way to Hampton, and leave me with fifty cents in my pocket when I got there."

The invitation to revisit his old home, to which

I have referred, and the welcome accorded him
there, formed, I am sure, one of the most gratifying incidents in Mr. Washington's life.   He
had left West Virginia an untaught, unknown
boy ; he returned the honored guest of the state,
city and people, with a reputation which is more
than national.   Ex-Governor W. A. MacCorkle,
the last Democratic governor of the state, and
Mr. Wm. M. O. Dawson, the secretary of state
of the Republican state administration, in office
at the time, met Mr. Washington at the train
with an open carriage into which he was taken
and driven to the place in the city where he was
to be entertained.   Perhaps only those who have
lived in the South can fully realize the signifi-
cance of this courtesy.   On the evening of the
day of his arrival the public meeting, of which
I have spoken, was held at the opera house.
Rev. D. W. Shaw, D.D., the colored pastor of
Simpson M. E. Church, presided at this meeting.
Governor G. W. Atkinson, the chief executive
of the state at the time, and ex-Governor Mac-
Corkle, with many state and city officials, sat
upon the platform, along with several prominent
Negro citizens.   A chorus of Negro children from
the public schools furnished music.   Ex-Governor
MacCorkle, in the preliminary speaking, said
that while the white men of the country had
been discussing the best methods by which to
solve the race problem, Mr. Washington had
grasped hold of that problem and done more to
solve it than any man living.   Governor Atkin-

son spoke of his life-long acquaintance with Mr. Washington, and closed by saying, " I introduce to you Booker T. Washington, formerly of West Virginia, but now of the United States." A reception and banquet were given Mr. Washington at the City Club rooms by the colored citizens; there were several less formal social functions, and Governor Atkinson gave him a public reception on behalf of the white citizens at the executive rooms in the State Capitol. From out of all this I find that one sentence from the prayer of a colored minister who opened the first meeting in the opera house is going to stay fixed in my mind longer than anything else. He thanked the Lord for having given the race "a leader with such a consecrated character *and so much practical common sense.*"

CHAPTER III.

" When I reached Hampton," Mr. Washington has said in telling of his introduction to that institution, " and presented myself as a candidate for admission to the school, the instructors who saw me first were not at all certain that they cared to enroll me as a pupil, a fact at which I do not wonder, as I remember the appearance I must have presented to them. It had taken a considerable time for me to make the journey over the mountains. I had walked a good share of the way, and had often slept in barns before I had occupied my lodging under the sidewalk in Richmond. My clothes had been none too good when I started ; they were much worse when I reached my journey's end. I wanted to stay, and pleaded to be allowed to do so ! I said I would work. They wanted to know what I could do. I told them what I had been doing. Finally one of the instructors took me to a room which needed sweeping, gave me a broom and told me to see how well I could clean the room. I suppose I swept and dusted that room as many as four or five times before I was satisfied with it. Then one of the lady teachers came and inspected my work, and reported that it was satisfactory. That was my entrance examination, I passed it successfully, and was allowed to stay."

Of his life at Hampton, Mr. Washington has said : " At Hampton I found the opportunity — in the way of buildings, teachers, and industries provided by the generous — to get training in the class room and by practical touch with industrial life to learn thrift, economy, and push. I was surrounded by an atmosphere of business, Christian influence, and a spirit of self-help that seemed to have awakened every faculty within me, and caused me for the first time to realize what it meant to be a man instead of a piece of property. While there I resolved that when I had finished the course of training I would go into the far South, into the Black Belt of the South, and give my life to providing the same kind of opportunity for self-reliance and self-awakening that I had found provided for me at Hampton."

The school at Hampton, Virginia, to which Booker Washington found his way over the mountains, was an outgrowth of work begun during the war by representatives of the American Missionary Association among the Negro refugees who had flocked to Hampton by thousands. In 1868 a regularly established school for colored pupils was opened as a result of this preliminary work. In 1870 this school was incorporated as the " Hampton Normal and Agricultural Institute." The first principal of Hampton Institute was the late General S. C. Armstrong, who for some time previous had been an official of the Freedmen's Bureau at Hampton.

In General Armstrong were combined a rare personal fitness and unusual preparation for the management of such a school at such a time. He was the son of Rev. Richard Armstrong, D.D., who for forty years had been a missionary in the Sandwich Islands, and for sixteen years minister of public instruction there. General Armstrong was born in the Sandwich Islands, and as a young man served under his father in the Department of Public Instruction. Later he came to New England, and having graduated from Williams College, in 1862, at once entered the army. He was soon promoted to the position of colonel of a colored regiment, remaining in the service until the close of the war allowed him to undertake the work of the Freedman's Bureau.

General Armstrong made Hampton a great educational institution. He devoted his life and strength to the work, from the founding of the school until his death in 1893. He was succeeded by Dr. H. B. Frissell, as principal, under whose administration the high standard of the school has been maintained. Thousands of Negro and Indian students have been trained there, and the influence of the institution for good is incalculable. Its graduates and students are scattered throughout the West and South. While Tuskegee is the most vigorous offshoot of the Institute there are other important schools in the South which have been established and developed by Hampton graduates. Among them are Calhoun, and Mt. Meigs People's School in Alabama;

Kittrell, in North Carolina, and Gloucester and Lawrenceville, in Virginia.

Mr. Washington graduated from Hampton in 1875, and the same year went back to his old home at Malden, West Virginia, to teach the school there, remaining in charge of this for three years. He brought to his work the new methods and practical ideas which he had learned at Hampton, and his reputation as a teacher survives in Malden to this day. One of the innovations which he introduced was that of having military drill by the boys of the school, using sticks for arms, since they had no guns. A man who was his pupil then, told me a story of this drill when I was in Malden. That the first manœuvres of his raw recruits might not attract undue attention, the young teacher was accustomed to assemble his company in a secluded spot back from the village, among the hills, where they would be out of sight. One day they were studiously drilling there, keeping step to the "hip! hip! hip!" of their instructor, when there came around a turn in the mountain path, squarely in their faces, a half-grown boy coming into town from his country home. He gave one frightened look on the advancing company, and then, throwing down whatever burden he carried, ran back home to spread a report that the war was on once more, and that he had met a company of advancing soldiers.

In 1878 Mr. Washington took a course of study in Wayland Seminary, Washington, D. C.

The next year, at the request of General Armstrong, he returned to Hampton as an instructor there, being given the care of the Indian boys who were then at the school.

In 1880, the member of the Alabama Legislature from Tuskegee, a prominent Democrat, and afterwards speaker of the House, offered a bill which was passed by the General Assembly, appropriating $2000 annually to pay the salaries of teachers in a normal school to be located at Tuskegee, for the training of colored teachers.

This act of the Assembly being approved in February of the next year, Mr. G. W. Campbell of Tuskegee, one of three commissioners appointed for the school by the legislature, wrote to General Armstrong, asking him if he could suggest a suitable person for principal of the new school. General Armstrong suggested Booker T. Washington, and recommended him so highly that eventually he was engaged. When Mr. Washington arrived at Tuskegee, he found no school house provided for him, and no prospect of any. The state had appropriated money to pay the salaries of teachers, only, and nothing for school building, furniture, books, apparatus and current expenses. All these the colored people themselves must provide if they would take advantage of the state's assistance.

In the first letter which he wrote to his Hampton friends, after he had arrived at Tuskegee, the new teacher said : " On Friday I rode about fourteen miles into the country to attend the closing exercises of the school of one of the teachers. From this trip I got some idea of the colored people in the country. Never was I more surprised and moved than when I saw at one house two boys, eight or nine years old, perfectly nude. They seemed not to mind their condition in the least. Passing on from house to house I saw many other children, five and six years old, in the same condition. It was very seldom that I saw any children decently dressed. If they wore clothing, it was only one garment, and that so black and greasy that it did not look like cloth. The colored teachers in this part of Alabama have had few advantages, many of them having never attended school themselves. They know nothing of the improved methods of teaching. They hail with joy the Normal School, and most of them will become its students. If there is a place in the world where a good Normal School is needed, it is right here. What an influence for good; first, on the teachers, and from them on the children and parents."

The first session of the Tuskegee Normal and Industrial Institute was assembled in 1881, on the Fourth of July, — an auspicious day for the beginning of the enterprise. There were thirty students in attendance, the most of them teachers like those whom Mr. Washington had described in his letter. One of the students was a colored preacher, the pastor of one of the churches in Tuskegee, a man fifty years of age. The problem of a school building was solved by an old

Negro church in Tuskegee being utilized for that purpose. The number of students increased rapidly, as the news of the establishment of the school spread throughout the state. Pupils kept coming from towns farther and farther away from Tuskegee, finding opportunities for board in the town. An old shanty near the church was occupied as a recitation room, and Miss Olivia A. Davidson, a graduate of Hampton, and of the Framingham, Massachusetts, Normal School, was secured as an assistant teacher. This second building was so poor that I have heard Mr. Washington say that when it rained the roof leaked so badly that one of the boys was obliged to hold an umbrella over the teacher in order that she might be able to go on hearing the lessons.

The newly-established school had been in operation only a few months when the "practical common sense," for which the Negro minister at Charleston was so thankful, led the teacher to decide that he could not secure the best results possible from his efforts so long as he was able to influence his pupils only during the hours they spent in the schoolroom. He wrote to a friend: "An institution for the education of colored youth can be but a partial success without a boarding department. In it they can be taught those correct habits which they fail to get at home. Without this part of the training they go out into the world with trained intellects, but with their morals and bodies neglected."

In addition to this, many of the students were so poor that they could not afford to remain at the school long enough to get much real benefit unless they could have some opportunity to work to earn money, or to help to pay their expenses. One after another would come to the teacher, after a time, to say that his little store of money was exhausted, and that he must go. I quote a passage from a letter of Mr. Washington's written at that time, in which he said : " I remember the day I came to Hampton with but fifty cents in my pocket, and was given a chance to help myself. Oh, that it were possible to give such a chance to these students."

Just at this time an old plantation, about a mile from Tuskegee village, was offered for sale. It contained one hundred acres of fairly good land, and on the land were a few small buildings. Five hundred dollars was asked for the place, but of this only two hundred dollars need be paid down. The young teacher of the struggling school saw the opportunity, and a bold idea came to him. He wrote to the treasurer of Hampton Institute, and asked him if it would be practicable to lend two hundred dollars to plant a Hampton seed at Tuskegee. The answer came : "To lend you Hampton school funds,— No. To lend you at my own risk,— Yes, and here is my check, and God speed you."

The two hundred dollars clinched the bargain for the land, and within two months were returned to the sender. In less than three months more

Mr. Washington was able to write to this friend : —

"TUSKEGEE, DEC. 18, 1881.

"Four months and a half ago, without a dollar of our own, we contracted to buy a farm of a hundred acres, at a cost of five hundred dollars, on which to permanently locate our school. To-day the last dollar has been paid."

How was this money raised ? Over a hundred dollars was secured in Tuskegee, by entertainments, and by subscriptions from both whites and blacks. A friend in Connecticut gave three hundred dollars. The vacation students at Hampton, the young men and women who remain at school through the long summer vacation to work to save money enough to go to school the rest of the year, gave nearly a hundred dollars from their hard-earned savings. About this time a friend gave one hundred dollars, with the stipulation that it should be used to buy a horse to work on the land, something the school greatly needed. This money was put into the hands of Mr. Lewis Adams, a colored man at Tuskegee, to expend. Mr. Adams had been prominent in helping to get the school established, and was one of the three commissioners originally appointed by the state to act for the school, a position which he has ever since held. He was a shoemaker and tinsmith by trade, and as soon as those branches of industrial work were established at the school he took charge of them.

He still remains at the head of the tinsmith department, and it was in the school's tin-shop that he told me about this first horse, on the occasion of my being in Tuskegee in 1899. " I took that one hundred dollars," said Mr. Adams, "and made it go so far that when I came back to the school I had a good horse, a second-hand lumber wagon, a harness, a plow, and a sack of corn to begin to feed the horse on. That horse did all our work for a long while." Now the Institute has six hundred head of stock, — horses, mules, cattle, sheep, and hogs.

So the new departure was made. The farm was deeded to a board of trustees who included representative men of the North and the South, white and colored, with a majority of no one sect. The preparatory class of the increasing school took possession of the old farmhouse on the plantation, and, as soon as the early southern spring made work on the land possible, the boys went to work with happy hearts to plant their first crops of corn and cotton.

CHAPTER IV.

THE accommodations for the school were much greater on the plantation than they had been in the town, but they did not keep pace with the demands made upon them. Before the first school year was completed it was necessary to make plans for a new and larger building. The corner stone of this building was laid March 30, 1882, at the celebration of the close of the first session of the school. The address on this occasion was delivered by Hon. Waddy Thompson, county superintendent of education. From a report of this celebration I quote a paragraph. This report, speaking of Mr. Thompson's address, adds, " With eloquent words he bade the workers Godspeed, trusting that their labors might prove a blessing to their race. A colored pastor present, feelingly exclaimed, ' I thank God for what I have witnessed to-day — something I never saw before, nor did I ever expect to see, — one who but yesterday was one of our owners, to-day lay the cornerstone of a building devoted to the education of my race. For such a change let us all thank God!'"

The report from which I have quoted says : " During the year, one hundred and twelve students from various parts of the state have attended the school, and now, during vacation, many of them are doing good work as teachers, by which to obtain money to return next year. By the aid of the people in Tuskegee, in money and labor, and by help from northern friends, the lumber is now on the ground for a new building, the building is being framed, and we are making every effort to have it completed by the beginning of the next session, September 1, 1882."

The new building, placed on the site of the old farmhouse on the plantation, was named Porter Hall, after one of the chief contributors to the building fund. It was a wooden building three stories high, with a basement, and contained six recitation rooms, a large chapel, a reading-room and library, a boarding hall, and, in the third story, dormitories for girls. Porter Hall was dedicated at the school's second anniversary, in 1883.

In the summer of 1883 a small frame cottage was put up at the school, containing four rooms, in which sixteen young men were lodged. Three rude cabins near the school were rented the same year, and in these thirty-six more young men found rooms, procuring their meals at the boarding department. A great advantage which resulted from this was that the boys who boarded at the school could work out a portion of their expenses.

The need for a dormitory building for the boys, which would accommodate at least a hundred students, was pressing. Mr. Washington, with an eye to permanency, decided to erect brick

buildings wherever structures of any considerable size were contemplated. Fortunately there
was a clay pit on the plantation, and he determined to have the young men make the bricks.

The work of preparation for the new building
went forward rapidly ; and the building was
needed. The winter proved one of unusual sever-
ity, and the temporary shelter provided for the
students was not always sufficient. On February
fifteenth of that year Mr. Washington wrote :
" Not less than ten hands went up in chapel a
few nights ago, in answer to the inquiry how
many of the young men had been frost-bitten
during the cold weather. The teachers were not
surprised at this ; on more than one night, when
making a tour of the rooms at a late hour to
give a comforting word when there were no
more blankets to give, the young men have been
found hovering around the fire, while the cold
wind poured in through the roof, sides, and floor
of the room. While there has been this suffer-
ing, so anxious have the students been to remain
at school that there has been almost no murmur
of complaint. They have shown cheerfulness
throughout. Must they be asked to endure the
same another winter ? We have faith to believe
not. They want nothing done for them which
they can do for themselves. They are now digging out the basement for the new building and
preparing the clay to begin moulding the bricks
as soon as the weather will permit."

A month later the teacher was able to write :

CLASS IN BRICK MAKING AT WORK.

" Our young men have already made two kilns of bricks, and will make all required for the needed building. From the first we have carried out the plan at Tuskegee of asking for nothing which we could do for ourselves. Nothing has been bought that the students could produce. The boys have done the painting, made the bricks, the chairs, tables and desks, have built a stable and are now building a carpenter shop. The girls do the entire housekeeping, including the washing, ironing, and mending of the boys' clothes."

One beneficial effect of the industrial work which came to be felt very quickly was the friendly intercourse which it brought about with the people of the town and county. When the Institute opened its brick yard it was the only place in the entire county where bricks were made. People who were engaged in building came to examine the bricks which the Tuskegee students made, and when they found they were good bricks wanted to buy them. The school soon found that it could have a market for all the surplus product of the yard. As soon as it was possible to do so a brick-making machine was bought and set up, and, now, for many years, the Institute has been selling several hundred thousand bricks every year to be used in the surrounding country.

During the first two years of the existence of the school, Mr. Washington had borne the heaviest part of the work alone. He had

attended to all the executive details connected
with establishing, moving and developing the
school. He had taught the scholars during
school hours in the schoolroom, and then had
taken the young men out on to the farm to clear
up the land and get it ready for the crops. He
had built fences, and driven the school's one
horse. He had directed the planting of sweet
potatoes and corn, and had superintended the
making of bricks.

In 1883 the Alabama Legislature appropriated
$1000 a year additional for the support of the
school, making $3000 in all, and Mr. Warren
Logan, another Hampton graduate, came to assist
Mr. Washington at Tuskegee. Mr. Logan has
been associated with the school since that time,
having now for several years held the office of
treasurer of the corporation, besides assisting
Mr. Washington in the executive work.

In the fall of the same year the trustees of
the Slater fund made their first large donation
to the school, $1000, with which to equip the
industrial department. Since then the benefits
received from this same source have been many
and generous. Up to that time the industrial
training had been chiefly on the land and in the
brick-yard. There was a small blacksmith shop
and wheelwright shop, and a printing office had
been established in which a small press was
worked by " man-power." With the help of the
Slater fund gift a carpenter shop was built, and
work at that trade begun, a windmill was set

WARREN LOGAN, TREASURER.

up to pump water to the school buildings, a
sewing machine was bought for the girls' industrial department, and mules and wagons were
bought for the farm.

The Slater fund is a sum of money left by
the late John F. Slater, a wealthy cotton manu-
facturer of Norwich, Connecticut. Feeling a
deep interest in the welfare of the South, and
realizing the value of industrial training to the
colored people, Mr. Slater gave one million dollars to constitute what should be known as the
John F. Slater Fund, the interest of which was
to be used in aiding such institutions as were
most effective in this kind of work. Dr. A. G.
Haygood, of Georgia, was the first agent of the
board of trustees to whom the management of
the fund was intrusted. Since his death, Dr. J.
L. M. Curry, of Washington, has held the position of agent.

In an address before the National Educational
Association, at Madison, Wisconsin, in 1884, Mr.
Washington said, "At the end of our first year's
work, some of the white people near Tuskegee
said : 'We are glad that the Normal School is
here, because it draws people here and makes
labor plentiful.' At the close of the second
year several said that the Normal School was
beneficial because it increased trade. At the
close of the last session more than one said that
the Normal School is a good institution ; it
is making the colored people of this state better
citizens. From the opening of the school to the

present, the white citizens of Tuskegee have
been among its warmest friends. They have
not only given of their money, but they have
been ever ready to suggest and devise plans to
build up the institution. When the school was
making an effort to start a brick yard, but was
without means, one of the merchants gave an
outfit of tools. Every white minister in town
has visited the school and made encouraging re-
marks. The president of the white college in
Tuskegee makes a special effort. to furnish our
young men with work, that they may remain at
school. "

Up to this time, Mr. Washington's talents as
a speaker had been exercised chiefly during the
summer vacation, for the raising of money among
the friends of the school in the North. This
address at Madison gave him rank as an educator of national reputation, and gave Tuskegee a
place among the educational institutions of the
country. Its effect in educational circles was,
to a great extent, what the address of the same
speaker at the Atlanta Exposition, in 1895, was
to the country as a whole. Mr. Washington
went to Atlanta the comparatively unknown
principal of a colored school somewhere in the
South. His address before that great audience
in the exposition buildings gave him a national
reputation and made Tuskegee almost a household word, a word to which interest will always
cling.

The school increased rapidly in size and im-

portance. Mr. J. H. Washington, the principal's
brother, who had followed him to Hampton and
had graduated from there, came to Tuskegee to
take charge of the industrial work. He now
fills the place of director of mechanical industries. Mr. C. W. Greene, also from Hampton,
came in 1888 as farm superintendent, and has
retained the place ever since. Among others of
the early teachers who have been constantly
connected with the school since they began their
work there, are Mrs. Logan, Mrs. B. T. Washington, who has charge of the industrial work for
girls, Mr. J. D. McCall, director of the academic department, Mr. M. T. Driver, the business agent, Mr. James N. Calloway, the manager of the Marshall farm, and possibly some
others of whom I have not been able to inform
myself.

I find an interesting description of the appearance, methods and plans of the school in those
early days, and of the conditions amid which it
worked, in an article written by Mr. Logan in
1884. From this sketch, to which the author
gave the title, " Life In and Around the School ;
from a Teacher's Standpoint, " I quote a few
paragraphs :

" It is sometimes asked, ' Does it pay to educate the Negro? ' Well, that depends, for him
as for others, upon how he is educated.

" An old colored man in a cotton field, in the
middle of July, lifted his eyes towards the heavens
and said : ' De cotton is so grassy, de work is so

hard, an' de sun is so hot, dat I believe dis dar-
key am called to preach.'

" There is no doubt that some of the would-be
teachers, as well as the would-be preachers, in
their desire for education are inspired, as some
of their brothers in white are, by a yearning, not
for usefulness, but for ease. Simply to gratify
them in this would certainly not pay for gener-
rous contribution to their education.

" But, if along with mental training, the Negro is taught that, as President Garfield told the
students at Hampton Institute, ' Labor must *be*,
and labor must be free, ' that in free labor is
dignity and prosperity and self-respect ; if with
his book learning he learns to respect the rights
of others, to do right from a love of right, and is
given some useful trade as a start in life, why
will it not pay handsomely to educate him ; to
make him an intelligent and useful American
citizen, instead of an ignorant and dangerous
one ?

" This is the work of the industrial school.
This is the work of Tuskegee, the very place for
our cotton-field graduates.

" The great need of the South is competent
school teachers and skilled mechanics. The demand for both is much greater than the supply.
Colored lawyers might perhaps be dispensed with
for a while, but colored teachers, able to use
both head and hands, are an actual present necessity.

" The great majority of our Tuskegee students

hope to become teachers among their people. Almost all of them come from the country and are good material. Visitors are struck with their splendid physical proportions. Most of them are stalwart, robust young people, well able to work their way in the world, and eager for an opportunity. They have had poor home training and it is necessary to teach them correct habits of living, but they evince an eagerness to learn that is as surprising as it is encouraging, undergoing, in many cases, much privation and discomfort to keep in school. It is gratifying to watch the change that gradually takes place in their personal appearance, in clothes and manners, and expression of face.

"The course of study as planned extends through four years, but few can complete it without staying out for as much as a year to earn money. We do not think they will lose by this in the end. We hope to graduate our first class next year. The course is thorough in English lessons, composition and reading, with studies in literature. It extends in mathematics through elementary geometry, and includes geography, history, civil government, with special study of the school laws of Alabama, book-keeping, some study of the natural sciences, mental and moral philosophy, vocal music and the theory and practice of teaching.

"As an industrial school Tuskegee regards its manual labor department, not merely as a means to secure education, but as a valuable

part of education. Work is required of all.
The boys are taught practical farming, carpentry, printing, brick-making, blacksmithing and
painting; the girls, sewing and housekeeping.
The school hopes to add other industries as it
becomes able.

"We do not find that the manual labor inter-
feres seriously with the studies. We believe
that in the long run it will be found far more of
a help than a hindrance, through its influence
upon character and habits of industry. Of course
it makes a busy day for students and teachers,
from the rising bell, at half-past five, and the
work bell, calling some after breakfast to their
work-shops or cotton fields, and others to the
morning study hour, to the bell for 'lights out' at
half past nine at night, when the sleep of the
laborer is sweet. A busy day; but Tuskegee has
work to do, and means to do it."

CHAPTER V.

THE reports from which I have quoted in the last chapter, and Mr. Logan's article, written in 1884, give a vivid picture of Tuskegee at that time, and an outline of what the school hoped to do. A description of the school, as one visiting it sixteen years later found it, will show what had been accomplished in that time.

The town of Tuskegee is the county seat of Macon county. It is situated southeast of the centre of the State of Alabama, in what is commonly known as the "black belt." It is forty miles from Montgomery, the capital of the state, and one hundred and forty miles from Atlanta. It is conveniently reached from the North by way of the Southern railroad, to Atlanta; and the Atlanta and West Point, and Western of Alabama, railroads, from Atlanta to Chehaw, Alabama, at which place the Tuskegee railroad, five miles in length, makes connection. Being on a through line of travel from the North to New Orleans, the facilities for reaching Tuskegee are excellent. The Southern railroad runs through cars from New York and Washington. The service is so satisfactory, both as regards time and accommodations, that I have always found it a pleasure to travel there.

Tuskegee is one of the oldest towns in the state. Its name is said to be from an Indian word, Tuskigi, and it is also said that when De Soto marched inland on his famous expedition he found an Indian village by this name on the same site. In Alabama the name of the town is invariably pronounced Tuskégee, with the accent on the second syllable, and the "g" hard, like the same letter in the word "geese;" but in other parts of the country I find a tendency to pronounce the word as if it were spelled Tuskyjée.

The village and school stand on high ground, from which, on almost every side, one may overlook miles of plantation land and forests of oak and pine. The location is attractive and healthful. The village, through which one passes on going from the station to the school, is typically southern. In its centre is the Court House, a time-stained building in which, if one happens to be in town at court time, may be heard good specimens of that legal eloquence for which the South has always been so justly famous. Around the grass-grown and shaded yard which surrounds the Court House, is a rusty iron fence. Facing the spacious square which surrounds all this, are the banks, stores and other business buildings of the town. The residence streets lead out from the square at right angles, and, standing back from these, in great gardens, where, at Thanksgiving time, roses and chrysanthemums are still in full bloom, are many fine old houses, in front of which lofty pillars support porticos so broad and high that often a more modern house might almost be put into the portico entire.

The grounds of the school are a mile beyond the town. The institute now owns twenty-five hundred acres of land. This is exclusive of twenty-five thousand acres of land donated to the school by the Federal government in 1899. This last-named property is unimproved mineral land, to be retained for rental, or sold, as the school may decide is the most desirable. The value of the property, exclusive of the mineral land, is between $300,000 and $400,000. There are forty-six buildings, counting large and small, all of which, except three, have been erected by the labor of the students.

The school grounds proper comprise about one hundred acres. At the right of the main driveway, as one enters the grounds, is Cassedy Hall, a three-story brick building originally used for the industrial classes, but now, since the most of these classes have been moved into the new Trades School Building, converted into a dormitory for boys. Adjacent to Cassedy Hall is another small brick building also used as a dormitory. Near these buildings the visitor may often see several piles of logs,— oak, pine and poplar, — many of them well towards three feet through. They have been cut on one of the school's timber lots, and drawn in for lumber. The building in front of which they have been left is the sawmill, and the strident "buzz-z-z" of a stout circular saw which comes from the building, shows that the mill is in operation. The young men who are at work there are learning the sawyer's trade as the one which they expect to follow in life. Adjoining the saw-mill, so as to obtain its power from the same engine, is the wood-working shop, fitted with the necessary machinery; the carpenter shop, with fourteen benches; and the carpentry and repair shop; with separate classes in each.

Back of the saw-mill is a building in which a class of young women are learning mattress-making and repairing, the making of pillows, and upholstery. They find plenty of work in keeping the furniture of the school replaced and in repair. Recently the school has discovered that the long, elastic needles of the southern pine, fragrant and healthful, when thoroughly dried are excellent for stuffing mattresses, and this material has been largely used. Adjoining the saw-mill on the other side is the engine-room, electrical plant, machine shop and foundry. In all of these, classes of young men are doing practical work which has a present value, and in doing it are, in most cases, learning the trades which they expect to follow in later years. Eventually all these industries will be moved to the opposite end of the grounds, where they will be accommodated in the Trades Building, when that is completed.

The first building on the left of the driveway is Science Hall, a handsome three-story brick building containing class-rooms, laboratories and several sleeping rooms for the teachers and boys. This building was erected after plans drawn by one of the instructors in the school. Nearly opposite Science Hall is Olivia Davidson Hall, a four-story brick structure in which are recitation rooms and sleeping rooms for the teachers and boys.

All of the larger buildings have ample grounds around them, shaded by trees and brightened by numerous flower beds. A northern eye is caught at once by the profusion of southern vegetation, the cacti, yuccas and palmettos. The entire care of the grounds, flowers, shrubs and trees devolves upon the department of floriculture and horticulture. Young men and young women who are learning these arts work regularly under the direction of thoroughly trained men, who are graduates of schools which have made a specialty of such studies. The orchards and vineyards of the school are young, as yet, but it has, in all, several acres devoted to fruit. In this connection it may be interesting to know that, during the summer vacation, the school operates a steam canning plant, for the double purpose of putting up its own stock of fruit, and teaching the art of canning to such students as elect to remain to work at it during the vacation. In a summer when there is a good crop of fruit the canning department puts up about five thousand gallons, using one gallon tin cans made in the school's tin shop. About one-half of this stock consists of blackberries, the berries being bought at an

average price of twelve cents a gallon from the
farmers' families, who bring them in from miles
around. The balance of the fruit consists of
peaches, pears, plums, apples, grapes and toma-
toes, raised on the place. None of the fruit is
sold; it is all eaten in the dining rooms by the
teachers and students.

Next beyond Davidson Hall, on the same side
of the driveway, is Porter Hall, a wooden structure, the first building erected. In it now are
the principal's and treasurer's offices, and the
offices of the heads of some of the departments,
several recitation rooms and a large general
study room. Back of Porter Hall is a group of
smaller buildings used mainly for girls' industrial
work; in them are the cooking classes, plain
sewing, dress-making and millinery classes. Two
of these buildings are interesting from the fact
that they are all that are left of the original old
buildings which were on the plantation when it
was bought by the school. The little, old, white-
washed cabins are very dear to those of the
teachers who have been at Tuskegee ever since
those early days, and have watched the growth
of the school into what is now almost a city in
itself.

A little farther down the driveway, and on the
opposite side from Porter Hall, is the Phelps
Hall Bible Training School, a large, three-story
wooden building with broad verandahs around it,
erected as a memorial building by a friend of the
school in New York. Near Phelps Hall is a

BUILDING NOW USED AS A LIBRARY.

PARKER MEMORIAL HOME.

wooden house which was the home of the principal for several years. Mr. Washington has recently moved into a brick house built just across the main road from the school grounds. The building of this house was largely made possible by the kindness of friends of the school in the North. It enables the principal to entertain, more conveniently than he could do in his former residence, many of the guests whom the institute's reputation attracts to Tuskegee as interested visitors. The building which Mr. Washington vacated is utilized now for a library and for reading rooms. _ Scattered about the grounds are several other residences in which other members of the faculty, including the chaplain and the doctor, live with their families.

Just in front of the library the driveway divides, and the right-hand section of it leads down past Alabama Hall, a four-story brick building, on the lower floor of which are the dining rooms and kitchens. In this building are the reading room, music room and reception room for the young women, and the rooms of the principal of the young women's department, Mrs. Bruce, the widow of the late ex-senator and ex-registrar of the treasury, B. K. Bruce. The upper floors of Alabama Hall are used for sleeping rooms for the young women. Beyond Alabama Hall are two large wooden buildings used as girls' dormitories. One of these is named Hamilton Cottage for the late Robert H. Hamilton who for several years led the famous Hampton quartette, and later led the Tuskegee quartette when they went North to sing to raise money for the school. Still farther on in the same direction is the laundry, a large three-story brick building, and Huntington Hall, a commodious brick dormitory for girls, recently erected with money given by Mrs. C. P. Huntington. In design and in finish this is one of the finest buildings belonging to the school. Near Huntington Hall is the girls' hospital, a small wooden building which should be replaced by a larger and better one, and the Parker Memorial Home. The last-named building is the gift of two friends of the school in Brooklyn, who, realizing that a great number of the young women who came to Tuskegee as students need home-training quite as much as any other form of education, provided this opportunity for such training. Many of these young women come from one-room cabin homes; few of them know anything of practical housekeeping. The Parker Home is a neatly designed and well-built wooden dwelling house. It contains a reception room, guest room, dining room, kitchen and laundry, all thoroughly and tastefully furnished. The remainder of the building is divided into sleeping rooms. This building is the home of the young women of the senior class during all of their last year at the school. In it, and from the care of it, they learn practical "home-keeping" with the help of attractive modern accessories. Occasionally, by Mrs. Washington's permission and under her guidance,

these young women are allowed to give little
dinners, teas and receptions, for which they make
all the preparations.

From Huntington Hall the grounds slope
down past the pumping station and reservoir,
through a beautiful oak grove, to a portion of
the farm land.

Returning to the main driveway in front of
Alabama Hall, and passing Willow Cottage, a
girls' dormitory, the next large building which
the visitor approaches is the Slater-Armstrong
Memorial Agricultural Building. This is a
handsome brick building containing laboratories,
museum, lecture rooms and recitation rooms.
In addition to its regular annual appropriation
of $3000 the State of Alabama now allows the
Institute $1500 a year additional for the support
of an agricultural experiment station, the work
of which is carried on by the school's agricultural department. Very near the agricultural
building are located the practice schools maintained as an adjunct to the normal department.
These schools are in charge of able normal-
training teachers. The pupils are the children
from the families of the members of the school's
faculty, and children from the town and surrounding country whose parents are glad to
avail themselves of the advantages of so good a
primary school. In this school the students in
the normal department teach a certain number
of hours each week.

Beyond the Practice School is the Slater-

Armstrong Memorial Trades' Building for boys,
the largest building on the grounds, and one of
the best.   The outside dimensions of this building are two hundred and eighty-three feet by
three hundred and fifteen feet.   It is rectangular
in shape, built around an inner court.   It is of
brick, with tin roof, finished throughout in yellow
pine, and is heated by steam and lighted by
electricity.   Except for the rear annexes it is
two stories high.   The plan after which it is
built affords all of the shops ample light and air.
The blacksmith shop is a fair sample of the
accommodations given the industrial classes.
That room is thirty-eight by sixty-one feet square,
lofty, lighted on three sides and fitted with an
exhaust fan for ventilation.   The shop contains
nine stationary forges, blowers, anvils, and all
the necessary tools.   Blacksmithing is a favorite
trade with the young men, and the shop's force
is always full.   An idea of the standard of the
work done here may be had from the fact that
many of the blooded horses from all over the
country are brought here regularly to be shod,
because the teacher in charge of the shop is such
an expert workman.   All of the indoor trades
for boys are accommodated in this building with
the exception of those which I have described as
being located near the entrance to the grounds.
On the opposite side of the driveway from the
Trades' Building for boys there is now being
built a similar building on a somewhat smaller
scale in which will be accommodated the girls'

industrial departments. This building is the gift of two friends of the school in New York, the same who two years before gave the money to enable the chapel to be built.

Near the trades' buildings stands the chapel. In years past the rapidly increasing number of pupils caused the school to outgrow one after another of the rooms which had been used for devotional exercises. For several years there had been used for this purpose — because it was the only building about the school into which all the students could gather at one time — a rude, temporary structure built of unplaned boards, with no floor but the earth and no seats but backless benches made by spiking planks upon posts driven into the ground. Recently money was given for a chapel and the students built it.

The chapel is built of brick, with stone trimmings. The plan is that of a cross, the dimensions being one hundred and fifty-four feet through the nave and choir, and one hundred and six feet through the transepts. The seating capacity of the auditorium is twenty-four hundred. All of the devotional services are now held in this building, the annual Negro Conference meets here, and it was in this building that President McKinley spoke when he visited Tuskegee. The building of this chapel illustrates, as well as any one instance can, the methods of the industrial training at Tuskegee. The plans for the building were drawn by the school's instructor in architectural and mechanical drawing. The bricks, one million two hundred thousand in number, were made by students in the school's brick yard and laid by the men in the brick-laying classes. The lumber was cut on the school's land and sawed in the saw mill on the grounds. The various wood-working classes did the work which came in their departments. The floor is of oak ; all the rest of the finish is in yellow pine, and the use of this wood in the lofty arch of the ceiling gives a particularly rich effect. The pews were built after a model designed by one of the students, and another student designed the cornices. The tin and slate roofing was put on by students, and the steam heating and electric lighting apparatus was installed by them, although this was the first building in which they did this work, these two trades being among the last which the school has been prepared to teach.

It should be remembered that at Tuskegee not only are all of the students Negroes, but also all of the teachers. There is no one connected with the school, except some members of the Board of Trustees, and one or two persons not resident at Tuskegee, who is not of the race which the school is designed to educate. With this policy to be followed it sometimes has been difficult for the school to find colored men and women thoroughly trained in the trades for which teachers were sought, a fact which would seem to point towards the need of more general industrial training for the people of the race.

SCIENCE HALL.

THE CHAPEL AT TUSKEGEE, BUILT BY STUDENTS.

Frequently the entire country has been canvassed to find capable instructors. Many of the teachers, especially of the older ones, come from Hampton. The director of the agricultural department is a graduate of the Iowa State Agricultural College. The teacher of horticulture comes from Ann Arbor. One of the teachers of cooking is from Mrs. Rorer's school in Philadelphia, and the instructor in gymnastics for girls is a graduate of the Boston Normal School of Gymnastics.

The Institute's barn having been destroyed by fire, the stock and farming tools were sheltered for several years in temporary buildings on a part of the grounds beyond the Trades' Buildings. Early in the year 1900, however, a sum of money with which permanent barns should be built was given by friends of the school in Brooklyn, and the erection of the buildings begun from plans drawn by Mr. R. R. Taylor, the same architect who designed Science Hall and the chapel. The buildings in this group are located on both sides of the road which leads from the school grounds to the farm land, and at a considerable distance from the other buildings. When completed they will comprise a poultry house, dairy house, dairy barn, horse barn, and piggery, on one side of the road, and on the other a slaughter house, and two large shelter barns for farming tools and wagons. Each of these buildings will be separate and at a considerable distance from any other. They will be modern in style and appointments, and will greatly add to the efficiency of the agricultural department and to the ease and profit with which its work can be carried on.

At some little distance from the grounds is the brickyard, the first industry started, and one of the most profitable. The clay in the pit is good and easy to get out. Improved machinery has been provided from time to time, until now two million bricks are made in a year. I have always remembered the pride with which, on the occasion of my first visit to Tuskegee, a student pointed out to me the difference between the rougher, hand-made bricks of which the older buildings were constructed, and the smooth, machine-made bricks built into the last new building which had been erected then. No artist exhibiting a picture which had taken a medal could have shown more pride in his work than did that young man in the neatness of that brick wall.

Outside the school grounds there has sprung up a good-sized village of dwelling houses, the homes of members of the faculty and their families. Some of these buildings are owned by the school and rented, but many of the teachers own their homes, with more or less land surrounding them. These houses, in style, furnishings and surroundings, would bear comparison favorably with the houses in the suburbs of any town. The main road of the county passes through this village. Over that road travel during the year, including those who come to Tuskegee at conference time, thousands of Negro men and women who live in the surrounding country. These people ride in all kinds of dilapidated vehicles, drawn by steers, neglected-looking horses and mules ; they wear clothes which are apt to be short in quantity and disreputable in quality. The majority of them live from hand to mouth, in one-room cabins built on mortgaged or rented land. Every time they pass through this village, or see Tuskegee's school buildings, they are obliged to have an object-lesson in what other men and women of their race have done — in what they themselves can do if they will but try. A journey back into the country in which these people live shows that some of them, at least, are profiting by the lesson.

CHAPTER VI.

BECAUSE Tuskegee affords such excellent facilities for industrial training, it should not be inferred that this side of the educational life of the Institute is emphasized at the expense of academic training. It is the aim of the school to have its system of moral and religious, mental and industrial education so balanced as to secure the best results consistent with the needs of each pupil.

Mr. Washington's opinion in regard to the relative value of industrial and academic education I have repeatedly heard him express in words similar to the following, which I quote from an address which I heard him make in Charleston, South Carolina:

"I would say to the black boy as well as to the white boy, get all the mental development that your time and pocketbook will afford, the more the better; but the time has come when a larger proportion — not all, for we need professional men and women — of the educated colored men and women should give themselves to industrial or business life. The professional class will be helped in proportion as the rank and file have an industrial education, so that they can pay for professional services.

"I would not have the standard of mental development lowered one whit, for with the Negro,

as with all races, mental strength is the basis
of all progress; but I would have a greater
proportion of this mental strength reach the
Negro's actual needs through the medium of the
hand."

Mr. Emmett J. Scott, Mr. Washington's private secretary, in a recent magazine article, has
said: "Tuskegee seeks to teach the dignity of
labor to its students, to afford them the best
possible opportunity for the development of their
mental faculties, emphasizes systematic industrial
training, and fosters the habits of right thinking
and right living. There are hundreds of schools
where colored students can receive literary training, but those in which young men and women
can learn trades, in addition to their literary
training, are very few."

If I give more space to a description of the
industrial side of the work at Tuskegee than
to any other, it is not because equal prominence
is not given to mental and moral and religious
training there, but because there are so few
schools where the trades, industries and agriculture are taught to colored students so thoroughly as they are at Tuskegee, and because
the industrial work there has as yet much of
the interest of novelty to students of educational
problems.

For the school year of 1899–1900, there were
enrolled at the Institute over one thousand students, who came from twenty-eight states and
territories, and from Cuba, Jamaica, Porto Rico,

Africa and Barbadoes. Naturally, more students
come from Alabama than from any other one
state; but nearly three hundred residents of the
state of Georgia attended the school in that year.
Florida, South Carolina and Texas always have
been largely represented among the students,
quite as many coming from those states as from
Mississippi and Louisiana. To teach and train
this number of students requires the services of
a faculty of nearly one hundred persons. A
visitor to Tuskegee cannot but be impressed by
the earnestness with which the teachers undertake their work, and by their devotion to the
manifold interests of the institution.

The requisites for admission to the Institute are
a good moral character, attested by recommenda-
tions from some reliable person, a good physique,
and a fair ability to read, write and cipher. No
student who cannot read and write is admitted,
and no student is admitted to any department,
on any terms, under fourteen years of age. The
school year is divided into three terms of three
months each. These are practically continuous,
as it has been found to be desirable to have the
most of the vacation time combined into one
long period in the summer.

The course of study is arranged primarily for
four years — preparatory, junior, middle and
senior; but because of the great diversity of
requirements among so many students, some of
whom come with almost no preparation, the preparatory grade is divided into three classes, A,

B and C, and the middle grade into two classes, A and B.

The members of the C preparatory class, the lowest, in their first year take arithmetic as far as common fractions, grammar, geography as far as the study of the United States, reading, spelling, music and drawing. The B and A classes of this grade continue these branches.

In the junior year the pupils have advanced in arithmetic to interest ; they continue the same studies as in the year previous, and begin United States history.

The members of the B middle class finish arithmetic and begin algebra, finish history and begin civics, and add physiology. Those in the A class of the same grade finish algebra and begin geometry, take book-keeping, geology, physics and chemistry.

The studies taken by the members of the senior class depend upon whether they elect to take the normal or trades' course. In the former, the studies of the final year are psychology, rhetoric, English and American classics, ethics, pedagogy, and a review of the English studies of the previous year. The trades' seniors have advanced chemistry, mechanical drawing, geometry, physics and trades' work.

The agricultural and mechanical work is carried on in connection with a four years' course in the academic department. Training is given in thirty industries, special effort being made to teach those which are most likely to be available in the South. The courses of study in the trades are as carefully graded and as consistently followed as are those in the academic department. It would make this chapter of inconvenient length if I were to give a full outline of the courses laid down in all these trades, and I therefore select only a few as samples : —

CARPENTRY — *First Year.*

Names and uses of tools; sharpening and setting for use. Working out pieces of timber to various gauges and lengths; straightening, squaring, beveling. Forming angles by halving pieces together, as applied in framing. Plain dovetailing, as applied in framing. Sketching and making plain brackets. Lectures on general topics. Study and construction of problems in carpentry. Observation lessons.

Second Year.

Framing. Inspection of brick work. Straightening, squaring and plumbing. Bracing, tying and bridging. Sizing studs, joists, etc. Formation of cornices. Setting window frames. Shingling and flooring. Weather boarding and boxing. Lectures and supplementary studies. Problems in carpentry. Selection of building sites and examination of building soils.

BLACKSMITH SHOP — *First Year.*

First Term : — Cleaning the shop. Making fires. Names of the tools and their uses. Care

CARPENTRY CLASS PUTTING THE ROOF UPON HUNTINGTON HALL.

of the tools and their places. The importance
of keeping water and coal in the troughs, also
economy. Striking. The different size drills
and how to run a drill press. The different size
stocks and dies, also how to cut threads. How
to keep shop in order. Compositions are written on these subjects weekly.

Second Term : — The use of the hand ham-
mer and tongs. The figures on the rule and
measurements. The different sizes of iron.
The formation of iron and steel. Welding iron,
also the different kinds of welds,viz. : Plain, jump,
dovetail, and also long and short laps and their
effects, and scarifying. The use of sand. Practice in making lap links, lap rings, staples, hasps,
S-hooks, gate hooks, hame hooks and round
rings. Resetting tires, and the use of the trav-
eler. Compositions are written on these subjects monthly, and monthly examinations are
given in all work.

Third Term : — The use of welding com-
pound. Welding steel, viz. : Spring, tire, axle
and tool. How to get the measurement on jobs
without the bed. Welding and setting axles.
Measurement of the track of axles. Welding
and setting tires, also dish of new wheels. Making clips, nuts, brace ends ; also welding braces
the proper length. Putting work together.
Bench work, viz. : Filing, clipping, jointing and
fancy work. The effect of sand and emery
paper on finished work. Compositions on these
subjects each month.

58   Tuskegee

Second Year.

First Term : — Horseshoeing. The condition of a shoeing floor. How to make a shoer's fire. The name and use of shoeing tools. What a mould is and how to make it ; also how to strike on a shoe. The names and sizes of shoes and nails, also the different kinds of shoes. How to file a shoe, how to pull off a shoe, how to trim a foot and clinch a shoe. The different parts of a foot and how to drive a nail. The different kinds of shoes that are used for horses with different ways of traveling ; also different shaped feet. Special lessons in fitting for special cases. Monthly compositions.

Second Term : — Wagon work, such as farm wagons, express wagons and platform wagons. Dash and rail work, and the different kinds and names. Fender work. Make different kinds of tools, also tempering. Work from drawings. Repairing different parts of buggies. Estimating cost of different articles, and jobs. Trimming up of jobs. Compositions monthly on these subjects.

Third Term : — Buggy gear work. Body and hoop work. Practice in truck and carriage forging. Different kinds of traps and their names. Talks on general work are given each day. Repair work of an advanced order is done by the students while this course is being taught.

During one of my first visits to Tuskegee, I

happened to be passing the blacksmith shop late one afternoon, and looking in through the door saw all of the young men in the shop gathered in a group, and so intent upon something in their midst, that I went in to see what it was that interested them. I found that they were gathered around an anvil which the teacher was using as a demonstration table, and on which he had placed the lower joints and hoofs of the hind legs and forward legs of a dead horse. With them he also had the articulated skeletons of similar members. Each hoof was dissected before the class, and while this was being done, it was easy to show the students just how a shoe should be nailed on in order to get the best effects, and how driving even one nail wrongly or carelessly might do great harm. It seemed to me as if this was a very desirable exercise for a young blacksmith to have, and yet I doubt if many apprentices in shop work get such lessons as this. At the time, I supposed that this was an exceptional occurrence which I had happened on by chance, but as I became more familiar with the methods of instruction at Tuskegee, I found that this was only a regular "theory lesson," such as is held in all of the trades' classes during the last hour of every afternoon, four or five days in the week.

The question may be asked, " Does the teaching of trades in such a school as Tuskegee give practical results?" It seems to me that it does, and I happen to have an illustration of what the

blacksmith class does in this line, which seems
to me to be interesting, and which came under
my observation entirely by chance.

I had gone to the town of Greensboro, Alabama, to see a young man who had graduated
from the tinsmith department at Tuskegee and
gone into business at Greensboro. When I
called at the house where this man boarded, he
was not at home, but a young colored man at the
same house, who heard me state my errand,
came forward and said, " I am from Tuskegee,
too. Won't you come in ? I am so glad to see
any one who has been at the school." Greensboro is between one hundred and one hundred
and fifty miles from Tuskegee.

I found on talking to this young man that he
had learned his trade in the blacksmith class at
Tuskegee, leaving the school the year before,
and had been in business for himself at Greensboro for very nearly a year. His name is William
M. Thomas, and his shop in Greensboro is on
Tuscaloosa street. As a boy, he had wanted to
learn to be a blacksmith, and a family of white
people in Greensboro, with whom he had lived
for several years, told him of Tuskegee, and
advised him to go there. He entered the school
in 1894, and remained four years, paying his
way by work while he was there. At the end
of four years he left school to go into business
for himself, and returned to Greensboro, where
the same friends lent him twenty-five dollars with
which to open a shop. From what he had earned

during the year he had paid this money back, had supported himself, and had bought and paid for a small house and lot of land. I might add here, what he did not tell me, but what I learned afterwards at the school, that he regularly sends a sum of money to the school as a gift, to help along the work. This, by the way, a great many of the graduates do, however cramped their means may be. This young man has a good shop, had two apprentices working for him when I was there, and had all the work he could do, almost all of it from white customers.

I happened to ask this blacksmith some question about the relative amount of work which he had done in two different months. "Wait a minute," he said, "and I will tell you exactly." He brought out an account book, and from it was able to give me, not only each month's business, but each day's, and could tell just what part of this was from shoeing, and what part was from repairing. From this he was able to explain why a falling off of forty dollars from September's work to October's did not mean that the regular work of the shop had suffered, but that the fact that the farmers were getting their wagons ready for the cotton crop had temporarily swelled the amount of work done in September.

What impressed this on my mind was his saying, as he closed the book, "I shouldn't have known how to do this if I hadn't been to Tuskegee. That is one of the things they taught us there."

"How do I feel towards Tuskegee?" he said, repeating my question, as if he wondered why I should ask it. "I feel towards Tuskegee as towards a father."

In the course of study for blacksmithing, quoted near the beginning of this chapter, it will have been noticed that at the end of each term's course there is added: "Compositions on these subjects each month." Some one may have said, on reading that, "What use?" While I was at Greensboro, talking with Mr. Thomas, who, by the way, was only a little over twenty years old when he went to work for himself, he said: "When I came back here and opened a shop a good many folks thought I was too young to know my trade; so I wrote a piece about horseshoeing, and had it printed in the local paper." At my request he procured for me a copy of this paper, the *Greensboro Watchman*, for April 19, 1899, in which the advertisement was printed. I imagine the advertisement paid for itself, without any doubt. I found it so interesting, for many reasons, that I quote it verbatim. It should be remembered that this man had very little education when he went to Tuskegee, that he paid his way by work during the four years that he was there, much of the time attending the academic classes only at night, and that he did not remain to complete the academic course. He is only one of many who have learned the same trade at Tuskegee, and are now doing equally good work for themselves.

Horseshoeing.

"Among the many trades of man these two stand high — blacksmithing and horseshoeing. Horseshoeing has been done ever since the horse has been trained to the use of man. The first shoeing that was known was made of rawhide, and tied to the foot. I do not know where it was tied, but anyway, it was used as a protection to the foot. Later on, when man advanced to a higher circle of civilization, science and art, he found, by the examination of a dead horse's foot, that the shoe could be made of iron and nailed on. I suppose the first man that discovered it was the first to nail it on.

"Now, up to this age of the day we have 159 kinds of shoes; and out of this number of shoes I have made forty-six kinds for one foot — for calking, ankle-skinning, knee-hitting, over-reaching, knuckling, corns, founder, stumbler, runner, keel-joint, dropped sole, seedy toe, and others which I shall not take the time to mention. For a man to be a successful shoer, he must know the shoes mentioned above, and their use. Many men call themselves horseshoers, but they do not know what a careful piece of mechanism a horse's foot is, and the least awkward lick will get it out of gear.

"A horse's foot has over two hundred different parts to it, and for you to shoe a horse right you must have them located.

"The bars of a horse's foot should not be cut ;

but nine-tenths of our smiths cut them away, not knowing what use they are. They answer the same purpose to the foot that joists do to a house. Many other things I would like to mention, but space will not allow me.

"I shall give you a light sketch of heavy shoes, and their abuse.

"For an example: Suppose a horse shod with shoes weighing two pounds each, and traveling at such a jog as to require him to lift his feet all around, once a second, or sixty times a minute, keeping up his speed for five hours, how much work does he perform — that is, how much does he lift? Lifting one foot sixty times a minute for four feet, 60 x 4 equals 240, lifting two pounds each time, in one minute he will lift 480 pounds, which multiplied by 60, will make in one hour, 28,800 pounds, and in five hours, 144,000 pounds, or 72 tons. This calculation is based upon the scientific experiments of thinking men of to-day. Hence it will be seen at a glance that these heavy shoes cause a great waste of energy, and further, that the weight of the shoes should be determined by the size of the horse.

WM. M. THOMAS."

Greensboro, Ala., April 10, 1899.

ROBERT L. MABRY, TAILOR.   JOSEPH L. BURKS, GROCER.

GEORGE F. BAKER, '99,   WILLIAM M. THOMAS,
SHOEMAKER.   BLACKSMITH.

CHAPTER VII.

EXCEPT for a small entrance fee, there is no charge for tuition in any of the departments of the Institute, because, almost without exception, up to this time the students have been too poor to be able to come to school if they were obliged to pay tuition. It is this which makes it necessary to look to generous friends outside the institution for a large share of the money required to meet the running expenses. The charge for furnished room, board and laundry, is only eight dollars per month. Small as this would make the aggregate expense in a year, fully half of the students are obliged to attend the night school for the first one or two years they are at Tuskegee, in order to obtain money with which to complete the course.

The day school is designed for those students who pay for their board, study in the day, and have six work days in a month — one day in each week and every other Saturday. Students are compelled to work on these days. Day students are given an opportunity to work out a part of their expenses, if they wish. With a good outfit of clothing, forty-five or fifty dollars is sufficient money to carry an industrious student through a school year of nine months. The rate of wages depends upon the amount

of work a student can perform, and the cash
value of the same.   At the end of each month
a bill is given to every student, showing what
he may owe the school, or what the school owes
him.

The night school is designed for young men
and women who wish to educate themselves, but
who are not able to pay even the small charge
made for board in the day school.   No student
is allowed to enter the night school who is under
sixteen years of age, or who is physically unable
to perform an adult's labor.   Students will not
be admitted who are known to be able to enter
the day school, and whenever a student has
fraudulently secured admission he is dismissed
from the night school and must enter the day
school or leave the institution.   When students
enter the school they are assigned work by the
director of industries.   Frequently students wish
to be given work at some special trade, and whenever this is possible it is done.   In assigning
students the director is guided by the individual's
natural ability, intelligence to grasp the trade,
and physical ability to perform the necessary
duties.   At the beginning of the school year it
often happens that certain industrial departments
are quickly filled, and students wishing to enter
these departments after that are given miscella-
neous work to perform until the desired vacan-
cies occur.

That their lack of money obliges so many of
the students to enter the night school, and to

work during the day, is probably no disadvantage to them in the end. Although nearly all of the young men and women who come to Tuskegee have been accustomed to work, and to work hard, before they come to the Institute, very few of them have had any knowledge of those methods of labor by which the best results may be obtained. The months which these young persons spend in systematic labor, under the careful direction of instructors who are skilled in the best modern methods of work, form as much a part of their education and as valuable a part, I believe, as anything they will learn from books.

Students having no previous knowledge of the trade at which they work are allowed to work out their board bill during the first six months. As their work becomes more valuable their wages are increased proportionately. No students except those who work at Marshall Farm are paid cash for their labor ; what they earn goes to their credit, to be drawn upon for their expenses after they enter the day school.

I mentioned in the last chapter a visit which I made to Greensboro, Alabama, to see a graduate who is in business there as a tinsmith and roofer. This man's name is William Pearson, and he has a shop on the main street of the town. He was a native of Lafayette, Alabama, who heard of Tuskegee through a student who had been at the school, and went there. The first year he worked on the farm and attended night school.

The next year he entered the tinsmith department. He graduated from Tuskegee in 1897, and after working in Opelika, Alabama, for a time, came to Greensboro and opened a shop for himself. He had already built up a good trade, nearly all of it from white customers. Among other work he had just completed a job on the roof of the Southern University there, one of the most successful white schools in the state. Greensboro, by the way, is the home of Lieutenant Hobson, and Mr. Pearson had not long before completed a job of repairs on the roof of the Hobson mansion, a beautiful old house surrounded by magnificent grounds. I asked this young man, also, how he felt towards Tuskegee. He said, " I feel that I owe all that I am to Tuskegee."

The course of study which this young man followed at Tuskegee, in common with all the members of the tinsmith class, was as follows :

First Year.

First Term : — How to keep the shop. Names of machines and how to use them. How to stop holes in old tin, and how to hold soldering cups to solder. How to turn burs and put on spring bottom. How to turn locks on folding machines.

Second Term : — To cut and make small cups and such other small vessels as can be made from scraps. How to do the soldering on neat and small vessels. Review work of first term.

Third Term : — To do heavy repairing, such

as putting in bottoms with double seams. How to make larger cups. How to make small pans. How to do important repairing.

Second Year.

First Term : — The difference in soldering heavy and light seams. How to make small buckets, large buckets, and flared buckets. Special attention given to the art of using the shears.

Second Term : — How to cut simple patterns. How to make large pans, such as milk pans, round cake pans and wash pans. How to make dish pans, slop cans, foot-bath tubs and coffee pots. How to make pans, buckets and cans in different shapes. The fluids used in soldering different metals.

Third Term : — The use of square and compass. How to get the different angles. How to cut patterns. How to put on tin roofs. How to make and put on conductor pipes. How to get the cost of work. How to work zinc, as in lining bath tubs and boxes.

In this course, as in most of the metal working classes, the last hour in the afternoon alternates between theory lessons and drawing. The wood-working classes also have practice in wood turning.

One of the departments which I have always found particularly interesting is the machine shop and foundry. At the time of my last visit to Tuskegee there were thirty-two young men

at work in this department. Six of these were
seniors, and were working their third and last
year in the shop; the others had been there a
shorter time. These men, when they go from
the shop after a three years' course of instruction and labor, will be thoroughly well able to do
general machine shop and foundry work, and to
act as engineers up to a rather high grade of
engine. In the latter branch of the work they
get a good deal more drill than do apprentices
in most machine shops, as the boys in the senior
class at Tuskegee take all the care of the engine,
each being in charge a week at a time. Several
graduates from this department hold excellent
positions, in different parts of the South, and a
large number of others are doing good work at
their trades.

The boys in the machine shop have built the
two engines which furnish the power in the
Institute's printing office, and also the two which
run the machinery in the laundry. The young
man who was running one of these engines in
the printing office, at the time, was a good example of the typical Tuskegee student. Two
years before he "had come out of the bush," as
they say there — that is, he had come to the
school from back on a plantation where he had
grown up with no opportunities whatever; had
never even seen an engine of any kind. Already,
two years had made a capable workman of him.

In addition to building the four engines which
I have mentioned, the students had recently

built a large steam pump which had just been
sold to be used in the country, and while I was
there they were repairing the broken machinery
of a large cane mill, the parts of which had been
brought several miles to the shop. In making
such repairs as this the Institute's shops are a
great convenience to the surrounding country,
as there are no other shops within thirty miles
which have facilities for doing such heavy work.
A part of the class were employed at that time
putting the plumbing into the bath rooms in a
girls' dormitory then in course of construction;
and the theory classes in the machine shop when
I attended their sessions were occupied with a
discussion of the questions which had come up
in connection with that work.

The course of study in the machine shop is as
follows : —

Students entering this department begin with
practice and theory in steam and water piping.
Instruction is given daily on the proper manner
of piping sinks, ranges, steam boilers, engines
and residences. Each student will have several
hours each week during work time for practice
in foundry work — preparing moulds for castings
of all kinds, making cores, drawing patterns and
cupola management. The course in machine
work will then begin with work on the bench
with vise tools ; chipping, filing, brazing, scrap-
ing and the laying off of work for power machines is practiced on the bench. The students
are then given work on an improved, back-

geared and self-fed drill, and instruction is given on the grinding of the various tools used on the machine. Work in centering, reaming, facing, counter-sinking and drilling to line is taken up. The use of the boring-bar, also the measurements and sizes of the standard United States taps, dies and drills for same, are taught on this machine.

Instruction is next given on the shaper, consisting of grinding shearing tools, and of plain, square, round and fancy shaping, with the use of the surface gauge, straight-edge, bevel square, micrometer, etc. Instruction on planer work, the management of belts, the use of various planing tools, planing straight, taper and angle cuts, the use of the boring-bar and center in planer work. Instruction in lathe work begins with the feeds, speeds, and the various tools in turning straight, taper, bevel and round work, drilling, reaming, centering, milling, grinding and screw-cutting. The use of the lathe tools, such as rests, back-gears, cross feeds, boring-bars, mandrels, arbors, center-indicators and micrometers, will be given.

Students will have an opportunity to design and construct some tool or piece of mechanism, and experiments will be made in steam engineering, the management of steam boilers, heaters, steam pumps, etc. Each class in the machine and engineering departments will be expected to design and construct, ready for use, some machine, pump, or engine, such as may be used

CLASS IN DAIRY WORK.

STUDENTS AT WORK IN MACHINE SHOP.

in the trade, during each term of their study, the drawings and specifications for the same to be submitted to the instructor for approval.

Something which one of the young men in the machine shop said one day amused me, and at the same time impressed me as an illustration of the great indirect influence which the school is all the time exerting, and which I believe is destined to be almost as great a power for good as the more direct results of the school.

Deficient in the conveniences for proper training as are so many of the homes from which the students come, it is essential that Tuskegee make a special effort to inculcate habits of personal cleanliness. Abundant bath rooms with an ample supply of hot and cold water are provided, and all of the students are obliged to bathe twice a week, and advised to bathe daily. Mr. Washington is an earnest advocate of what he calls the " gospel of the night shirt and the tooth brush," and many are the practical talks which the students hear, under suitable conditions, upon these and similar topics.

I was talking one day in the machine shop with a young man who was then in his first year as a student at the school. He had come from a home a considerable distance away — in .another state, in fact — and had been telling me about his life at home and his present plans.

" But, say! " he broke out, after a moment's pause, " I had worn a night shirt, nights, for over a year, before I came here. It was like this, " he explained, " " A fellow whom I had always known, who was a student here, came home for vacation. He was telling me about the school, and among other things, he told me that all of the fellows here wore night shirts, and told me what good things they were. After he was gone back, I thought to myself that if night shirts were such good things, I'd better try them. So I went and bought me a pair and began to wear them, and say ! I wouldn't have been without them since for twice the money. "

CHAPTER VIII.

FOR some time after the Institute was established the students as a general thing were not anxious to learn trades. They were glad to work while at the school, but it was as a means to an end and not for the sake of what the work would teach them. Often the parents who sent them wanted their children "taught books." The last five or six years have seen a change in this respect. Now, almost without exception, the students wish to learn a trade, and the applications for places in the trades classes are often more than the school can accommodate.

I asked Mr. J. H. Washington, the director of industries, what he thought had brought about the change. He said : " Formerly the majority of the students wanted what they called ' a nice job,' one in which they could be, as they said, ' gentlemen.' Money was no object. Now, partly from the teachings of the school, I think, and partly from observation, they are coming to have a very different idea with regard to work. They have found that it is not necessary for a man to be dirty, simply because he works at a trade or on the farm. They are coming to see, too, that a man can hope to have little recognition unless he has some tangible results to show for his labor."

The favorite trade at present seems to be

tailoring ; at least there are more applications for entrance into this class than to any other. About thirty young men and ten young women can be given instruction in this department. The course of study requires two years. Wheelwrighting, machine-shop work and blacksmithing are also trades which attract large numbers.

One only needs to see the work to know that it is practical. Hearing a sound of hammers one day, as I was passing a building which was being converted into a boys' dormitory, I went in to see what work was being done there. Four young men were laying floor — laying a good floor, too, Three of these were in their first year at the Institute. They were working under the oversight of the fourth, a young man in his second year of study. While I was in the building, one of the instructors in carpentry came in to see how the work was going on. He had squads of men at work like this, in half a dozen places, and divided his time among them.

In the carpenter shop, a little distance away, several members of the class were at work making the door frames and window frames to be put into Huntington Hall. The brick masons had completed their work on this building a few days before, and the carpenters had taken it in hand. Just at that time the men in one squad were engaged in putting on the roof, and when I went through the yard in front of the carpenter shop, late that afternoon, I found the theory class in that department taking up for their lesson

that day the laying out of a roof — pitch, length
of rafters, and similar problems. The young men
were gathered around the instructor, where he
had placed some boards upon a pair of wooden
horses in the yard, and first one and then another,
with try-square and pencil, would lay off a plan
of a roof from the dimensions given him.

These theory classes are utilized in all the
trades, for the answering of questions which may
arise during the day's work, and for the instruction which these questions suggest. I have always found these classes extremely interesting.
In the saw mill, that afternoon, I found the class
practising grading lumber, learning to see quickly
the various imperfections in a stick and to distinguish into what grade they would require that
the lumber be sorted. There were seven young
men in the class, all of them of such superb
physique that I was divided in my admiration
between the ease with which they handled the
heavy timbers and the interest which they took
in the classification of the lumber.

In the foundry the class — twelve young men,
all beginners — were having a lesson in the making of " cores " for castings. The South is very
generally a country of fireplaces, and one of the
simplest problems for these new students in the
foundry is to cast "andirons." The students in
the machine-shop take founding in their first
year's work. It falls to the lot of some of the
members of this class to work in turn at firing
the boiler and running the engine at the pump-

ing station, a building some little distance from the rest of the school buildings. I was returning from a walk, one morning, and passing near the station saw the boy whose business it was to work there, and another boy, so absorbed in the contents of a skillet which they were heating at the door of the fire-box that they were quite unconscious of my approach to see what they were cooking. When they did see me it was to greet me with a welcome so hearty that it showed they were not doing something which they ought not to do, and they at once set to work to show me how they were making the castings for a small — very small — steam-engine which they were planning to build. They had whittled out the patterns, and made their moulds in a little box of sand, and now were melting " Babbitt metal " with which to make their castings. I remained long enough to see the liquid metal poured into the moulds, and although I had a fear that this particular engine would never "run," I have little doubt that some day these same young machinists will build one which will.

Coming in from the same walk, I found near Huntington Hall a rough "practice" fireplace, which one of the beginners in bricklaying had been building there. The teacher of brick masonry had let the boy build it there, where he could instruct him while he was overseeing the more advanced students at work on the walls of Huntington Hall. The ways like this in which time and opportunities are utilized are endless.

From Ocober to March of each year one of the most skillful students in brick work goes to Tuskegee town three evenings in a week to teach the trade to such colored men there as may wish to learn, but who have not time to spare except in the evening. The class meets in a room which Mr. Washington hired for that purpose, and usually from eight to ten men avail themselves of the opportunity.

That Mr. Washington practices what he preaches in regard to industrial education may be seen from the fact that his own son is learning the brick mason's trade. When this boy was ten years old he began regular work, a certain number of hours each week, with the mason's class. I saw him when he was fourteen years old laying brick in the walls of the new Huntington engine and boiler house, and I had seen, previously to that, an excellent job of repairing a break in a plastered wall which he had done in the house in which his father then lived. I heard Mr. Washington say, in a public address in New Orleans, in referring to this: "I do not know that my boy will be a mason when he grows up; he may be a doctor or a lawyer or a minister, for all I know; but this I do know — he will have a good solid trade to fall back on if he needs it."

One of the very practical departments of the school is that which teaches harness making, saddlery and carriage trimming. In a country where nearly a half of the going about is done on horseback and on muleback, as is the case in many parts of the South, the trade of saddle making acquires an importance which in the North it does not know. This shop not only makes and repairs all of the school's harnesses — no small task where between fifty and a hundred horses and mules are driven and worked — but has a good trade in making harnesses and saddles for sale. The school's carriages, too, of various patterns, are trimmed in the same shop. The course of instruction which the pupils have in this department here includes : —

First Year.

First Term : — Care of shop. Names and care of tools. Thread-making and practice stitching.

Second Term : — Quality and preparation of leather. Names and dimensions of straps. Repairing all grades of harness.

Third Term : — Cleaning and oiling harness. Making odd parts of harness — such as hame straps, shaft tugs, bridle fronts, side straps, crupper docks, girths, etc. Fitting and finishing up harnesses.

Second Year.

First Term : — Review of work of first year. Names and grades of trimmings. Names and grades of leather. Economical cutting of leather.

Second Term : — Care of patent leather.

Stitching of patent leather. Cutting patterns. Making fancy harnesses — such as coach, buggy, truck, and all grades of express harnesses.

Third Term : — Review of work done in first and second years. Finishing work. Making all grades of cart and gig saddles. Inspection and criticising by the students of all work done in the shop. The course in carriage trimming is entirely separate from this.

I went into the harness shop one afternoon when the theory class was in progress, intending to remain only a few minutes ; but I found the work there so interesting that I spent the whole hour there. A part of the class, beginners, were having what might be called a competitive examination in blacking and polishing pieces of straps, to see which had best mastered the art. Another boy was making a crupper dock, and showed me how he stuffed it with flax-seed, so as to make it at the same time flexible and solid. The crupper dock this boy was making was to replace one which had been eaten by a rat with a tooth for flax-seed, and the spoiled part of the harness was utilized to show the members of the class the need of keeping a harness hung up when not in use, and the danger of throwing it down upon the floor of a stable. Other boys were called on to demonstrate how to make a "turn back," for a driving harness. Three boys were called up for this before the teacher was satisfied with the result. The third boy's explanation was as clear as could have been any student's demonstration of a problem in geometry. The strip of leather must be of just a certain length and width, to begin with, and then split, trimmed, and stitched in certain places in just such a way. All of the demonstrations were practical, the students in their heavy aprons standing around one of the large work benches in the shop.

One of the members of the harness-making class was a young Cuban, one of ten students from that island who had then been at the Institute about four months. When these students came only one of them could speak any English, but they had learned rapidly. They all were enrolled in some of the industrial classes of the school, getting an English education and a trade at the same time, with a view to returning to Cuba, fitted to meet the new conditions of life in that island. Mr. Washington said to me about these Cubans at the school, in reply to a question which I asked him : " My idea is to give these students industrial training, with the thought that they will return and become leaders in industrial work among their people."

What the director of industries had said to me about the students coming to understand that a man can work at a trade or on a farm and still keep himself neat, frequently came back to my mind in the evening, as I watched the students in chapel. The chapel services are held in the Institute church every evening at 8.20. All students attend, unless previously

A GROUP OF CUBAN PUPILS AT TUSKEGEE.

excused, and the members of the faculty attend very generally also.

Imagine a lofty, spacious church, beautifully finished in native woods, and brilliantly lighted with electric lights. A thousand young colored men and women sit facing the platform. On the platform are the teachers, and in the gallery just behind is a choir of over a hundred voices, with an organ, a piano, and an orchestra for instrumental accompaniment. Professor Charles G. Harris, the school's instructor in music, directs the choir. The service is simple: music, a prayer, a Bible selection, and a text for the day, recited by the leader and repeated by the school in concert. When Mr. Washington is at Tuskegee he conducts the service. His Sunday evening talks to the students have always been a feature of the school; they have been heard now by thousands of young men and women, and treasured up, to be used as guides in later life. When Mr. Washington is not at the school Mr. Logan takes his place. If there are visitors at the Institute they frequently speak to the students at this time for a few minutes. Sometimes there are announcements to be made or some general instruction to be given to the school as a whole. This opportunity is also utilized to drill the students in a body in chorus singing. Tuskegee has always striven to maintain and teach the beautiful, old-time plantation hymns, and there is hardly ever a service at which one or more of these is not sung.

I have sometimes heard Mr. Washington say at chapel: " Has not some one a new song to-night, which we can learn ? " Sometimes he has to repeat the request two or three times before anyone has courage to respond. Then, far back in the house, some single voice chants, half tim-idly at first, the words of a hymn which per-haps had never been heard before outside the backwoods church or cabin home where the singer had learned it. The quaint, high-pitched melody rises and falls — a voice alone — until a dozen quick ears catch the theme and a dozen voices are humming an accompaniment. The second time the refrain is reached a few voices join in boldly, a hundred follow, and then a thousand, sending up into the arches of the roof such a volume of sound as one is rarely permit-ted to hear. Mr. Horace White, the editor of the New York *Evening Post*, wrote of this music, after he had visited Tuskegee and heard the stu-dents sing: " Nowhere in the world, in non-professional ranks, have I heard their equals in musical gifts and training."

At the chapel services the young men sit on one side of the house and the young women on the other. The two main entrances to the church are at the front corners. The pews are so arranged that a broad aisle leads from each of the entrances down to the ends of the platform. These aisles are connected by one which passes directly in front of the platform and by another parallel to this, in the rear of the room. When the service is finished the leader nods to the young woman at the piano. She strikes a chord as a signal for attention ; another, and the young women rise ; another, they turn to position, and then, keeping step to the music of the orchestra, begin to march out. It is not a simple matter, though, this marching out, for the line starts far back by the door and the young women come slowly, two by two, down the long aisle to the stage, across in front of the stage, up the other side aisle, across the room again at the rear, and then, having completed a square, out at the entrance by which they came in to the service. Meanwhile, as if it were not a sufficiently trying ordeal to file slowly around the room in this way, with the eyes of all the rest of the audience fixed upon them, the young woman who teaches the girls gymnastics takes her station at the foot of the first aisle, as the column starts to move, and inspects each student as she passes before her. If a girl does not carry herself erect, or if any detail of her dress or general bearing is not absolutely satisfactory, the hand of the teacher stops her and she has to fall out of line and stand there in the eyes of all, embarrassed and humiliated.

When the girls have marched out the piano is struck again, and the boys rise and begin to march in the same way, going around the auditorium in a direction opposite to that taken by the girls. Major Ramsey, the instructor in military drill, meets the boys at the foot of their

aisle, and perfect indeed must be the deport-
ment and dress of the boy who gets past him.
Untidy hair, unbrushed clothes, dirt, unblacked
shoes, a button off or even a button of a coat
left unfastened, and out of the line the unhappy
culprit comes. Even after the teacher is passed
the ordeal is not over, for Mr. Washington or
Mr. Logan conducts a second inspection of the
line as it passes his place on the platform.

The result of this is that one will see nowhere
a neater or more neatly dressed company of
young people than the students at Tuskegee
Institute. In whatever work they may have
been engaged during the day, its traces have
been removed before they come to chapel, or,
for that matter, before they come to their supper,
two hours earlier in the evening.

I think that a prominent southern white man,
who understood Negro character thoroughly,
expressed the best comment on this when he
said to me, not long after watching for the first
time that nightly march in Tuskegee chapel : " I
am impressed by the philosophy of it all. Here
are a thousand Negroes, and not one of them
with a button missing or unfastened. I never
saw its like before."

CHAPTER IX.

I QUOTE a portion of one of Mr. Washington's Sunday evening talks, selecting the one which he gave on the evening of February 4, 1900. He chose for his subject that night : —

WORK

" It is an important thing to learn to get happiness and even information out of what one often calls the common and rather repulsive things of life. One of the most interesting books that I have ever seen was a book written describing the beautiful things which a person can find in a common mud-puddle — in a common hole of water, such as you see on the roadside, during the summer time especially. Now you would be surprised if you were to make a careful investigation, to make a careful study, how many really charming things one can find in a stagnant pool of water. The individual who has really the supreme art of getting happiness, getting useful information, out of everything that is in nature is a very happy individual; and that is what education is meant to accomplish — to enable one to get that which is beautiful, to get inspiration, to get real happiness out of the common things of life — everything : out of grass, out of trees, out of animals — everything. When a person can learn to get happiness, information, out of what we term the common things of life, that person has learned a great deal, and it is one of the last things that an individual, one of the last things that races, are inclined to learn. Now, I am going to speak to you to-night about one of the common things of life. It is common because it occupies so large a proportion of our time. I am going to speak about work — a very common word.

"You will find that the average individual spends, or is supposed to spend, perhaps about one-third of his time in some form of work. There are some individuals who spend ten hours, some twelve hours, or rather some think that they spend ten or twelve hours in some form of labor. Now, here is a thing that occupies our energy, our mental activity, in so large a degree that we ought not to count it an insignificant thing. A thing that occupies one-third or one-half of our life is something that should be important to us as individuals — it is something that we cannot lay lightly aside, it is something to ·be looked closely into. Now the question that would arise in the mind of any individual who thinks on the subject is, how to get the greatest benefit, the greatest amount of happiness, the greatest amount of that which adds to real life — to permanent growth — out of work. You can plainly see, if you are engaged in something that occupies such a proportion of your life, and you are not getting real growth, it is a serious matter. You spend a very large proportion of your time in sleep. Perhaps about one-third of your time is spent in this way, and you spend one-half of the remainder of your life in work, and if you are not getting real strength — when I speak of strength I do not mean only mental and physical; I mean strength of the soul as well, for it is the real object of all labor — you should find out the reason.

" If you are not gaining strength you are getting weaker, and the question I want to ask is, Are you getting real happiness — are you getting growth out of your work ? Whether it is purely mental, or partly mental and partly physical, or whether it is both mental and physical, are you getting growth, are you getting strength out of your work — are you getting strength of soul? If you are not getting happiness out of your present work, there is something wrong, and you want to stop and examine yourself, and see if you cannot so shape your life that you can get ıeal happiness out of every day you put in work, whether you are a student or whether you are engaged in any other form of labor.

" In the first place, there are two kinds of workers. There is the one class that is constantly seeking how little it can do, day by day. The first thing this individual thinks of before he gets out of bed in the morning is : How many things can I shirk to-day? What is the least number of hours that I can possibly seem to be engaged to-day and still get my pay? How can I leave off this thing and still get my pay?

Now that is one class. The other class is the
one that is constantly asking : How much time
can I put in this day? How much of real
work, of real effort, can I put in to-day? I
shall take it for granted that all of you belong to
the latter class, because it is the individual who
belongs to the first class who is constantly dis-
satisfied — who is constantly without a position.
It is impossible for an individual who is constantly studying to find out the least amount
of work that he can do, to get any happiness out
of any kind of labor. The happiest people I ever
saw are the people who find that the day is too
short.   I heard a man say the other day that he
was going to see if the jewelers could not construct a clock that registered thirty hours instead
of twenty-four hours.   He could not find time
enough in one day to do all the good things
he wanted to do. He belongs to the latter
class to which I referred. Now you want to
consider, in order to get happiness out of your
work, that whatever has fallen to your lot to do
is just as important as the work being done by
anybody else. No matter whether it is seen
by the outside world or not — whether anyone
knows of it except yourself or not — whether
it is scrubbing or plowing or making an axe-
handle — you want to consider that work just as
honorable, just as ennobling as any work that
can be done ; do not consider that work any less
important. I believe that the work the latter
individual is doing is just as important as the

work of any other individual. The work that every one of you is doing is important, and you want to consider it important, and you cannot get satisfaction out of your work unless you decide that it is important. The world will not be as complete to-morrow as it would be without the work being done for which you are responsible. You cannot get real happiness out of work unless you put intelligence and thought into it. See if you cannot improve to-morrow on the work that you did yesterday, and improve on it the day after to-morrow. Put earnestness into it; be sure to see that it is done as well or better than anyone else can do it; do it so well that no one can improve upon it; forget yourself in it. That is one of the ways to get the greatest happiness out of your work. Get so baptized in your work, so immersed in it, that you will forget yourself. Those are the people who get real satisfaction out of their work. Then, put your conscience into it. Do it just as well at midnight, if your work falls at twelve o'clock in the night, as you would at four o'clock in the morning — do it just as well as if it came twelve o'clock in the day, whether you are doing it in the sight of one hundred persons or doing it in a corner.

"Now, again, to get happiness out of your work you must prepare for it. You must begin to-night to think about the work that you are going to do to-morrow. The more perfect you do your work to-morrow the more perfect the

world will be. Plan for your work to-morrow ;
see how far you can put your mind into it. You
will find, if you will go on working in the
way that I have tried to advise you to-night,
that the most of the troubles that now confront
you will disappear. How am I going to find a
position, or keep that position, will cease to be a
question with you. If you will follow the advice
that I have given you there will be no trouble
about you getting or keeping a position, because
you will put yourself in demand — the world
cannot do without you ; so valuable will be your
occupation that the world will feel that it cannot
get along without your services. Such a person
need not be bothered about his position.

"Now if you are not getting happiness out of
your work it is your own fault ; it is because you
are not putting inspiration into it — because
you are not putting your conscience into it.

" The point I want to leave with you is, that
you will not only get physical strength out of
your work, but mental strength as well ; because
the people who are the strongest physically and
mentally are the people who get the most happiness out of their work. Above all, you will get
soul's growth out of work if you will only put
happiness into it, and you will only get happiness
out of it by following the plan that I have tried
to lay down to you to-night."

CHAPTER X.

ABOUT one-third of the students at Tuskegee
are young women. In the academic department
they attend classes with the young men. In the
industrial department type-setting, tailoring, caring for the sick, market gardening, poultry raising, bee-keeping, horticulture, and floriculture are
taught to both men and women. Among the
industries taught only to the young women are
mattress making, plain sewing, dressmaking and
millinery, cooking, laundry work, and general
housekeeping.

Caring for the sick is work for which the
students have shown a marked preference and
in which they have been very successful. In
one year, when I was at Tuskegee, there had
been sixty applications to enter this class, and
only sixteen pupils could be accommodated, the
Institute's hospitals being smaller and less con-
venient than the buildings in almost any other
department. The full course of study requires
three years, and is very thorough. During
their senior year in the nurse-training department the students are frequently employed by
the physicians at Tuskegee to take charge of
cases for them, obtaining much valuable experience in this way. This department has at no
time been able to supply all the demands made
upon it, especially during the months of the

Cuban war.   One graduate is now in charge of
the surgical ward of a hospital in Montgomery,
another is head nurse in a hospital in Mississippi,
and a third is employed as nurse in the white
young ladies' seminary in Tuskegee, one of the
most successful institutions of learning in Alabama.   While I was at Tuskegee a request was
received for a nurse to accompany a young
white woman on a two years' voyage around the
world.

Very many of the girls, when admitted to the
sewing classes, are absolutely ignorant of the
simplest principles of needle work.   The first
year's work consists of the most common kinds
of stitches, patching, darning, and general mending.   A large number of girls work in the various divisions of the seamstress classes.   They
not only make the girls' uniforms, and all the
sheets, pillow cases, table cloths, napkins, towels
and such articles as the school needs, but they
also mend the boys' clothes, no small task.   The
housewife of an ordinary home is often said to
sit dismayed before the mending for the family.
Think of being responsible for the mending of
the clothes of several hundred stout and vigorous young men!

The course in plain sewing requires two years.
In the second year of the course the students
make simple garments, such as skirts, under-
clothing, overalls, and colored shirts.   Students
who complete this course satisfactorily, or pass
an examination in plain sewing and the ability to

GIRLS LEARNING PLAIN SEWING.

make simple garments, are admitted to the dress-making classes. The course in dressmaking is carefully graded, and requires three years to complete. It is as follows: —

First Year.

First Term : — Choice of materials. Drafting and cutting foundation and outline skirts from measurement.

Second Term : — Making, hanging, draping, and trimming the skirt. Talks on forms; line and proportion in relation to draping and trimming.

Third Term : — Drafting, cutting, and fitting plain basques, and the general finish of these garments.

Second Year.

First Term : — Drafting basques, sleeves, and the different accessories to the basque from measurement. Drafting basques with extra seams for stout figures.

Second Term : — Cutting and fitting close and double-breasted garments. Cutting and matching striped, plaid, and figured basques and skirts. Talks on forms, including artistic and hygienic principles of dress. Talks on the subject of color and textiles as applied to dress.

Third Term : — Advanced work in making complete dresses from different materials.

Third Year.

First Term : — Cutting, fitting, and pressing.

Practice in the use of colors. Talks on the manufacture of cloth.

Second Term : — Drafting jackets of various styles ; making various styles of collars and pockets ; lining and finishing pockets.

Third Term : — Draping garments of every kind. Making and finishing garments of every kind from different materials.

In these departments, as in those in which the young men work, the students are paid according to the value of their work. The uniforms for the young women, made by the dress-making class, consist of a plainly cut, dark navy blue dress, trimmed with three rows of red braid about the skirt, and a red belt. Ties, ribbons, or other adornments about the throat must harmonize in color with the braiding on the dress. A black sailor straw hat with a white band completes the uniform.

All of the girls except those in the two lowest classes have at least two lessons each week in cooking. These lessons are practical work, the numbers allotted to each division being small enough so that each member of the class gets individual instruction. Special courses are arranged to teach the preparation of food for the sick. Particular attention is given to the correct arrangement of the table for different meals, to the proper methods of serving food and waiting on the table, and to table manners in general.

Not long ago I heard Mr. Washington say in

public : "How often has my heart been made to sink as I have gone through the South and into the homes of the people, and have found women who could converse intelligently on Grecian history, who had studied geometry, who could analyze the most complex sentences, and yet could not analyze the poorly cooked and still more poorly served corn bread and fat meat which they and their families were eating three times a day. It is little trouble to find girls who can locate Pekin or the Desert of Sahara on an artificial globe, but seldom can you find one who can locate on an actual dinner table the proper place for the carving knife and fork or the meat and vegetables." The course of study in cooking as taught at Tuskegee aims to meet the needs of such conditions as these.

Fifty young women work in the laundry. Three hundred thousand pieces are washed and ironed in this department each year. The building has excellent modern machinery, much of which it may be interesting to know was bought with money contributed for that purpose by young women who have graduated from the school. As it is realized, however, that few of the young women will have the assistance of machinery in their laundry work after they have left the school, the girls are trained in all the methods of hand work. The work which the laundry does is proving to be among the most practical and helpful of that done in any of the departments. There are many cases similar to

that of a young woman who found herself at the
close of the school year obliged to borrow money
with which to get home for the vacation. She
had had one year's instruction in the laundry.
When she reached the village where her home
was she found that she could have all the regular
work at washing and ironing that she wished to
do. Before the summer vacation was over she
had paid back the money she had borrowed, and
saved quite a sum towards her expenses during
her next year at the school. Another young
woman, who when she came to the school and
was assigned to work in the laundry was so
ignorant that she did not even know how to fold
a pocket handkerchief properly, came to the
teacher when she returned to the school after
her first vacation and said, " Oh, Miss Mabry,
when I was put to work in the laundry I didn't
like it a bit, at first, but I am so glad now that
I stayed there. When I reached home this
summer I found that I could have all the work
that I could do, at good pay ; and in this one
vacation I have earned more money than I ever
did before in my whole life."

It is intended that every girl who comes to
the school, whatever her regular work may be,
shall have as much training in general housework as is possible. One needs only to observe
the majority of Negro country homes as they
may be seen from the car windows of a train
passing through almost any part of the South
to realize the wisdom of this. All of the young

GIRLS LEARNING MILLINERY.

women at the school are divided into three classes, and each class does practical housework for three months in caring for the buildings of the school. I quote a paragraph from the course of study, which speaks for itself : —

" Spring house cleaning ; when to do it. How to do general weekly cleaning ; care and cleaning of lamps. Bed room ; where it should be located ; how to ventilate, light, and heat ; when and how to clean ; decorations suitable to be used. Beds ; when and how to clean ; when and how to air them ; why aired ; when and how to change bedding ; how to keep it through summer season. Sweeping and dusting ; how to sweep and dust properly ; how to build a coal fire ; when and how to burn out chimneys ; use of dust brush and pan, and trash box. Scrubbing ; how to use the brush ; advantages of brush ; how to remove paint ; how to polish window panes."

The provisions for teaching scrubbing recall Mr. Washington's address before the White Rose Mission, in New York, where he said : " I have often thought, especially when traveling from city to city in the North, what a good thing it would be to establish a chair in some strong university for the science of scrubbing — yes, the common, homely art of scrubbing. Seldom do we see clean floors ; the art seems to have passed away."

The training of young women in poultry raising, market gardening, bee-keeping, horticulture, and similar arts is in a measure a result of a visit which Mr. Washington made to the famous Woman's Agricultural College at Swanley, England, when he was abroad, although he had for some time previous to that desired to broaden the Institute's course of instruction in outdoor work for women. He has said in regard to this : " In our Southern climate there is no reason why women cannot be trained to do successfully many things which come under the head of agriculture, just as is true in many parts of Europe. These courses are designed to fit the girls for earning a pleasant and profitable living, and making the home tie more sacred by the application of the knowledge obtained. The courses of study are given in connection with academic training, and when satisfactorily completed certificates will be issued in connection with the academic diplomas." These courses of study are so interesting and so practical that I quote the first year's work in several of the classes : —

Dairying. — Fall term. The home dairy is taken up and a clear knowledge obtained of the kind, use, and care of dairy utensils, and of gravity creaming. A study of stone, wooden, and tin churns, ripening of cream, churning, working and salting the butter, preparing it for the market and marketing it. The feeding and care of dairy cows. — Winter term. The distinctive features of the commercial dairy are taken up. Separators, of which the school has two varieties ; churns, of which there are several patterns.

Feeding and care of the dairy herd. Breeds of dairy cattle and their selection. Butter making in larger quantities; salting, packing, and preparing for the market. — Spring term. Milking. A study of pastures. How to destroy lice and other parasites. The care of calves. The utilization of waste products of the dairy. Library work.

Poultry Raising. — Fall term. The economic value of poultry on the farm. Pure and mixed breeds. Plain poultry-house construction. The making of nests, yards, and runs. — Winter term. Special study of breeding and feeding. What kinds of eggs to set, and when and how to set them. The best breed of fowls to set. Management of the incubator. Period of incubation. An introductory study of young chickens. General poultry keeping and the saving of eggs for market. — Spring term. A more advanced study of young poultry. Brooders. Sanitation of the poultry house. Egg testing. Moulting and its effects upon different breeds.

Horticulture. — Fall term. The importance of an orchard and of small fruits. Varieties best suited to the localities in which particular students live. Selection and preparation of ground. Setting out and trimming. Extermination of borers, lice, scale, etc. Kinds and proportionate number of peach, pear, apple, plum, and fig trees, and of grape vines and strawberry plants which should be planted in home orchards. — Spring term. Spring planting. Trimming,

budding, grafting, spraying.　Care of grape vines.
The vine and post system of supporters.　Spring
layering and cutting.

Floriculture and Landscape Gardening.— Fall
term.　A study of common door yards, laying
out and beautifying the same.　The kind, care
and use of tools used in floriculture and landscape gardening.　Trimming and shaping of
beds and borders, and the general care of shrubbery and flowers.　The gathering and saving of
seeds.　Special treatment of rose bushes and
shrubbery.— Winter term.　Trimming of beds
and borders.　Mulching, tying, wrapping, and
preparation of plants for the winter.　Winter
decoration of grounds.　The decorative value of
native shrubbery.　A study of window plants,
their value in the home, in halls, and in public
buildings.　Their economic value. — Spring
term.　Renewing of beds and borders.　Sowing of seeds.　Propagation by layers, cuttings,
and divisions of roots, bulbs, corms, etc.　Kinds
of fertilizers for this special season and how to
use them.

Market Gardening.— Fall term.　The value
of the home garden.　Selection and preparation
of the ground.　Kinds of tools, their use and
care.　Planting, gathering, and marketing of fall
vegetables.　Gathering of seeds.　Drying pump-
kins, cushaws, okra, and fruits.—Winter term.
The selection of suitable sites for hot beds ;
making of beds, cold frames ; planting and caring for the same.　The raising and marketing of

GIRLS LEARNING FLORICULTURE AND LAWN GARDENING.

winter vegetables. — Spring term. Preparation
of the ground at this season. What seeds to
plant and how to plant them. Particular attention given to the production of early vegetables
both for the home and for market. Reproduc-
tion of plants by seed and by division of members.

These studies mean practical work. In the
dairy the girls make butter. In the poultry
raising department the girls do all of the work,
even to whitewashing the hen house and fences.
They feed the fowls, tend the incubator, and
feed and care for the chickens and ducks. The
school has about fifty swarms of bees. The girls
take care of these. In the market-gardening
class they have proved especially expert in
transplanting seedlings, and in gathering and
sorting seeds. They learn to handle a hoe
lightly and skillfully, to prune trees and shrubs,
and to care for the flower beds. Along with
this practical work they have class-room instruction, with a special view to bringing them to
understand the economic details of the work.
They are taught to distinguish between breeds
of fowls and varieties of plants which can be
raised with the most profit under certain conditions and in certain places. They have their
account books, and keep track of what profit or
loss there is in raising different breeds of fowls
and different varieties of vegetables.

CHAPTER XI.

FROM the time when industrial education was first established at Tuskegee, agriculture has been looked upon as one of the most important industries to be taught there. Probably eighty-five per cent of the several millions of Negro men and women living in the South must of necessity continue to live on the plantations and obtain a living from the cultivation of the soil. Mr. Washington, I know, believes it best that they should do so. I have frequently heard him say to audiences of his race: " Stay on the plantations. There is room there and a chance to work. Too often the young men and women who leave the farms to crowd into the cities find it very difficult to get work there. The idleness which results is almost sure to cause poverty and disease, if not immorality and crime."

The conditions under which a majority of the Negro farmers and a large part of the white farmers in the South labor are often pitiable. In many cases the farmer owns no land, and as a result must rent a "patch" on such terms as he can make with the landlord, to whom he contracts to deliver a certain portion of the crop for rent. He has little or no money with which to purchase supplies in advance, and so, before his crop is even planted, he has to mortgage the balance of it to some merchant in town for food for

himself and family to live on through the spring
and summer. As cotton is the readiest cash
crop in the country, neither landlord nor merchant wishes to make an advance on any other
crop. As a result, the farmer too often is
forced to plant only cotton — buying even his
corn meal and bacon of the storekeeper, and of
necessity obliged to pay almost any price which
the dealer may demand. The farmer knows nothing of the best methods of farming. Often he
works hard, and makes his family work hard, too,
but he does not understand how to make the work
count. Instead of concentrating his time and
strength upon a small area, on which he could
raise a paying crop, he struggles to half-till
twenty, thirty, or even forty acres with one
mule, and fails to raise a profitable crop on any
part of the ground. Even if the rent account
and the store bills are kept with absolute fairness
— and sometimes it is possible they are not —
the farmer frequently cannot figure them ; when
they get tangled he is helpless. The result in
too many cases is that when fall comes and the
crop is harvested the farmer finds that it is
already eaten up, and even if he and his family
are not "closed out"—that is, turned out of
their miserable cabin, and their few belongings
sold for debt — they have nothing left to live
on through the winter, and must exist as best
they can until the coming of another spring
makes it possible to mortgage another unplanted
crop.

In many cases it is the sons of such men as
these who come to Tuskegee. What are some
of the things which the school aims to teach
them? To get to own land, even if it be ever
so little, on which a man can raise such crops as
he chooses, and from which he need not move
from year to year. To cultivate a little land
well, instead of much poorly. To raise every
article of food possible, and to go without all
those not absolutely essential which he cannot
raise, until he has the money to pay for them.
To learn to utilize the natural resources of the
country — fruits, nuts, and forage — now almost
wholly neglected, and to improve the dairy,
poultry yard and hog pen. To acquire sufficient
education so that he may be able to plan out
what he wants to do, to keep account of what he
is doing, and to understand if he has done what
he ought.

The school owns in round numbers twenty-
five hundred acres of tillage land, pasture, and
wood land. About six hundred acres of this are
cultivated by student labor. A large number of
students are employed upon the land regularly,
while others work there a part of the time.
The greater part of these work there because
they expect to be farmers later in life, but it
frequently happens that students assigned to the
farm at first, because there is no other work
available at the time, and who then have no
intention or wish to become farmers, are so
attracted to the work as it is carried on at Tus-

TRADES BUILDING AND A PART OF THE DAIRY HERD.

kegee that they decide to remain in the agricultural department, and to make farming their life work.

In 1897 an excellent building was erected to accommodate the agricultural department, largely through the assistance of Mr. Morris K. Jessup, and an increased allowance from the Slater Fund enabled the work to be broadened. This building is named the Slater-Armstrong Memorial Agricultural Building. At its dedication there were present Hon. James Wilson, the Secretary of Agriculture, Hon. Joseph F. Johnston, the Governor of Alabama, and Dr. J. L. M. Curry, of the Slater Board of Trustees. The director of the agricultural department is Prof. George W. Carver, a graduate of the Iowa State Agricultural College.

The laboratory work which the department does is simple, and easily understood by the students. It consists largely in an analysis of the different soils, for the purpose of learning what elements need to be supplied in order to make them more productive and better fitted for the crops which the farmers of the South wish to raise. Fertilizers and feeds are tested in the same way, to determine which of them can be used to the best advantage. The average yield of sweet potatoes from an acre in that locality is less than fifty bushels. Experiments made by Professor Carver have shown that two hundred and sixty-six bushels of these vegetables can be raised from an acre, proper fertilizers being used.

The same acre of land the next year, with no fertilizer, produced a bale of cotton, whereas a third to a half a bale to the acre, as cotton is raised in that part of the country, is often reckoned a fair yield. One of the most promising experiments has been that of feeding acorns to stock. The school now buys a thousand bushels of acorns each year to feed out. The orchard and market garden are maintained for practical results. Budding, grafting, trimming, and the care of trees and plants are taught with a view to supplying the school with fruit and vegetables.

All of the scientific knowledge is carried daily into the fields and into the practical work of the various departments of the farm. Mr. C. W. Greene, who for almost the entire period of the school's existence has had charge of the work in practical agriculture, superintends the young men in the actual work of raising food supplies required by the needs of the school, and thus the technical instruction which they get in the laboratory and lecture rooms is worked out on the land. I have repeatedly been impressed by the interest which many of these young men take in the different branches of the farm work. It is no unusual thing for a student to come and ask to be allowed to work over-time in some other department than that in which he is regularly employed, for the sake of the experience which he can get. Mr. Greene and the men who are at the head of the various divisions

of farm work, such as stock raising, the care of
the dairy herd, the dairy, and horticulture, have
their regular theory classes, as in the other
trades, and one has only to attend one of these
classes and note the eager questions of the
students and the attention which they pay to the
instructors' explanations, to decide that they are
getting benefit from their studies.

Stock raising, and the care of stock of all
kinds, is a branch of the work in which the
students have careful instruction. The school
owns a herd of about one hundred excellent
cows, and all the details of dairy work are carefully taught. A visitor to the school has only
to have eaten the miserable white butter which
is so common in country districts in the South,
and then compare it with that which the Institute's dairy makes, to realize the value of this
course of instruction. The dairy when first
established was situated in the basement of the
agricultural building. I have been in the habit
of going into the dairy frequently in the morning
to watch the classes at their work. The stables
— to begin with — are kept scrupulously neat
and clean. Young men milk the cows, weigh
the milk, and deliver it at the dairy. Others,
in spotlessly clean white overalls and jackets,
separate the cream from the milk, using one of
the latest improved separators for this purpose.
Instruction is also given in the care of milk and
cream in small quantities, as in a country dairy,
where a separator would not be available. Other

young men and young women do the churning,
wash, salt, and pack the butter. Then they
wash, scour, and dry the utensils, and clean the
dairy. On any sunny day — and most of the
days in Alabama are sunny — there may be
seen put out in the open air on a platform back
of the agricultural building an array of shining
dairy ware which it would do a housewife's heart
good to look at.

A story which Mr. Washington is fond of
using as an illustration in his talks has to do with
this dairy :

" It came to our knowledge," Mr. Washington
says, " that the owners of a certain creamery
wanted to hire a superintendent. We had recently graduated a man who was perfectly capable
of filling the place in every way, but he was just
about as black as it is possible for a man to be.
However, we sent him on to apply for the position.

" When he made his appearance before the
owners of the creamery, they said, ' A colored
man ? Oh, that would never do, you know.'

" The applicant for the position said, very
politely, that he had not come to talk about his
color, but about making butter. His hearers
said it was out of the question to think of hiring
a colored man for the place.

" Our graduate still declined to talk about any
color except butter color, and similar details of
dairy work. Finally something which he said
attracted the attention of the owners of the
creamery, and they said he might stay for a two

weeks' trial, although they still assured him that there was no possibility of a colored man being hired.

"Well, the first week's make of butter was shipped, and when the returns came back — would you believe it ? — that butter had sold for two cents a pound more than any product of that creamery had ever before sold for.

"The owners said to each other : ' Now this is very singular ; ' and waited for the next week's returns. When that week's product was heard from it was found that the butter had sold for a cent a pound more than that for the week before — three cents more than the creamery's best record before our man had taken hold of it !

"This time the owners of the establishment did not stop to say anything. They just put that extra and unexpected dividend into their pockets and hired that colored man to run the creamery for a term of years. Three cents a pound extra on the price of the butter which he could make had knocked every particle of black out of his skin, so far as they were concerned."

The dairy furnishes all the butter, cream, milk, and buttermilk which the school and families of the teachers consume. Cheese is made at certain times in the year, so that the members of each class can have instruction in the art of making it. One experiment which Professor Carver made with cheese interested me. It has been rather commonly believed that the climate of Alabama is unfavorable to the keeping of cheese, and that therefore this branch of dairy work cannot be profitably carried on there. To see if this is true Professor Carver once, when making cheese, set aside a ten-pound full-milk cheese to experiment with. No especial care was taken of this cheese, except that occasionally it was turned over and brushed off. It was kept on a shelf in one of the lecture rooms. Several times it was carried out to farmers' institutes as an object lesson. One day I was in the lecture room and happened to notice it. It was then two years and two months old. I said : " I wonder what it would taste like," and Professor Carver, remarking that it seemed to have been kept long enough to satisfy the requirements of the experiment, proposed that we cut it. We did so, and found it delicious. Such work as this has a very practical value. The Negroes of the South as yet get little real benefit from dairying ; and yet in Alabama cows can be bought very cheaply, and can be pastured out of doors for almost the entire year.

Only a part of the Institute's land adjoins the school grounds. Marshall Farm, a plantation of about eight hundred acres, is three miles distant. Thirty young men are employed on this farm, under the direction of the farm manager and two resident teachers. The young men work upon the land during the day and attend regular night school in the big old house which was once the " mansion-house " of the plantation. When I was at the farm in the fall of

GRINDING SUGAR CANE AND BOILING SYRUP, AT MARSHALL FARM.

1899 the men were finishing the digging of thirty acres of sweet potatoes, and were piling the crop in the field to be kept for winter consumption. They had also raised twenty acres of sugar cane. The cane had been harvested from this ground and grinding was to begin immediately. About fifty barrels of syrup would be made that year — the season has been too dry for a good crop. The syrup would be consumed at the school, as, in fact, are all the products of the farm.

All food crops which can be grown profitably in the South are raised by the school. Many acres are devoted to vegetables and garden produce. Students who remain in this department for the two years' course become familiar with all the essential details of farming and are competent to take charge of almost any plantation. Those who remain for the full scientific course of four years add to this the ability to teach the science of agriculture, while even those who are not able to complete a year at the school carry back to their farm homes new ideas and habits of systematic, intelligent work which cannot but be of great benefit to them.

CHAPTER XII.

I HAVE always found it interesting to talk with individual students at Tuskegee — to learn something of their history, how they happened to come to the Institute, what they were doing, and what their plans were for the future. A few pages from one of my note books, repeating the substance of some of these conversations, will give a good idea of the average Tuskegee student. These are not exceptional cases in any way, or picked students, except as I picked them up anywhere and began to talk with them. My experience has been that something of interest could be written about almost every one of the students at the school.

Charles P. Adams, of West Baton Rouge Parish, Louisiana — about one hundred miles from New Orleans : " I heard of Tuskegee from a young man who had received a catalogue. I was twenty-one years old. I could read and write a little, and had learned to do a few 'sums.' I lived with an uncle and worked with him. We had bought one hundred and sixty acres of land — one hundred and ten of it cleared land, and the rest cypress swamp. This cost us $2800, and we were allowed four years in which to pay for it. We paid for it in the required time, by hard work on that portion of it which we cultivated, and by renting some parts of the balance.

One-third of this land is mine. It is good land, suitable for raising cane and corn.

"We got the last payment made on the land just after I came of age. Then I made up my mind that I wanted to get a better education before I settled down. At first my uncle discouraged me. He said I owned a good plantation; what more did I need? But when he found that my mind was set on it he agreed that I had better go, and gave me $70 to start with. That is all the money I have had, except what I have earned here. This is my fourth year at the school. I have stayed and worked all of the vacations, and have also had work on the farm and as a janitor.

"I cannot begin to make anyone understand my delight when I first saw Tuskegee — the beauty of it; and then later, when I began to understand and appreciate the system which prevails here. Then it was that I came to realize the needs of my folks at home. I shall stay five years in all. The thing constantly before me now is to go back, and in some way help the people around my home, and at the same time build myself up. My uncle is glad now that I came. I had a letter only a little while ago from him, in which he urged me to make the most of my opportunities here, 'because,' he wrote, 'when you come back a great deal will be expected of you.'

"One great thing which I have learned here is the value of 'system' in farming — to know just what you want to raise and how much land to cultivate. Then take that much land and make the most of it. Then I have learned to experiment. If one of two pieces of corn in different soils does the best, try and find out why, and from this know what to do the next year. Then I have learned economy. Our people at my home have a good chance to save. Any colored man can buy land down there, and the land is of the very best quality. They always raise more than they need, but they don't take care of the surplus. We can have a good school there just as well as not."

This man's studies at that time were physics, algebra, grammar, ancient history, geometry, and bookkeeping. I asked him what advantage some of these would be to him if he were going back to the bottom lands to be a farmer.

"They give me general development," he answered promptly. "To put it briefly: 'They help me to catch hold of things.'

"Tuskegee has done a great deal for me," he concluded. "It showed me how little I knew. I was so ignorant when I first came here that I just didn't know how ignorant I was."

Isaiah Hardeman, of Clinton, Kentucky, five hundred and fifty miles from Tuskegee, had just $5.10 when he decided to start for the school. "My father is dead," he told me. "My mother has one other boy, younger. She owns a house and a little land, and could spare me. She wanted me to come.

A DEMONSTRATION IN MILLINERY.

CHARLES P. ADAMS, A TYPICAL TUSKEGEE STUDENT.

" I was at the railroad station one day, trying to think of the best way to start, when a man came along whom I had once worked for in another town. He asked me what I was doing there, and I told him I was trying to go to Tuskegee. He was in some way connected with the railroad. He was going about a hundred miles on the line and took me with him. He left me at Jackson, Tennessee. I got some railroad maps there, studied out the way, and began to walk. I had walked about forty-five miles when I came to a place in Bethel, Tennessee, where there had been a smash-up on the railroad. They wanted all the help they could get to clear away the wreck. I took hold and worked, and for what I did I got a ride to Artesia, Mississippi. From there I walked again, making about twenty miles a day, until I had gone over a hundred miles. I had the bad luck to strike a locality which was quarantined on account of sickness, and had to walk around it.

" Then I got a job cording wood for a railroad agent, and worked for him until he gave me a ticket to Montgomery. I had money enough left to pay my fare from Montgomery to Chehaw, from which place I walked to the school. I got there so late at night that everyone had gone to bed, and as I did not know where to go I slept on the steps of the agricultural building."

I can imagine the first men out in the early morning — probably the milkers going to the barn — finding the newcomer asleep on the

steps, and saying as they passed him : " Here's
another."

" After I woke up," this young man continued,
" I inquired where I could find Mr. Washington
and was directed to the office. He had not
come then, and so I waited for him. My clothes
were not very good. While I was waiting for
Mr. Washington one of the young men at work
in the office gave me a suit of his own old clothes,
and two shirts."

It has always been a mystery to me how the
teachers at Tuskegee manage to retain a reason-
able amount of clothing. Such cases as this are
constantly occurring, to appeal to their sympathy,
and just as constantly the wants of the needy
ones are supplied by some one.

This young man was nineteen years old at the
time I was talking with him. He worked the
first year and went to the night school. In the
first vacation and by some extra work he made
enough money so that during his second year
he could enter the day school. For three
months he worked in the dairy, getting up at 4
A. M., so as to learn that work. During the vacation he cultivated a " practice garden," in
order, as he said, " to see if I had learned anything in the class room about gardening." This
garden proved so successful that the department
was credited with several dollars' worth of produce which came from it. He expected to stay
at the school two more years. I asked him what
he meant to do after he left the school.

" I intend to be a farmer," he said. " I think now of going to Oklahoma. Of course I've got to work somewhere, at first, to get the money to start with for myself. I don't know just where, yet ; but I'm going to do it somewhere."

The distance this young man walked to get to Tuskegee was nothing unusual. A great many of the students walk long distances to get there. December 23, 1899, two young men — Clarence C. Jeter and Thorney Evans — arrived at Tuskegee after having walked from their homes in Santuck, South Carolina — five hundred miles distant.

Augustus Neely, of Newberry, South Carolina : " I came to Tuskegee in 1895. I was nineteen years old then. My father was a blacksmith, and I came to the school with the intention of learning the machinist's trade. I had no money, and for the first two years I had to work days and go to the night school. In that time I saved $103. That, and what I could earn in vacation and by odd jobs, has been enough to keep me in school these two last years. In the winter I have charge of the steam-heating apparatus for heating the chapel.

" I expect to stay here six years in all, because my education had been so limited before I came here that I was very backward. After I get through here I want to work somewhere a year, so as to earn money enough to enable me to spend one more year as an apprentice in some very large shop. Then I will be ready to go to work."

This man already had a certificate as a steam engineer, and Mr. Thomas, the instructor in charge of the machine shop, told me that he was a capable workman.

I asked this man when he found time to get his lessons, when he was working all day and going to school at night. He said : " It is hard work to find time enough to study. You have to pick your time — nights, mornings, in the dining room, whenever you can get a minute."

This man is the oldest of a family of eleven— five brothers and five sisters. His next oldest brother had followed him to Tuskegee, and was a student there at the time of which I write. I asked him if all of the eleven were coming, and he said, " I hope so. I'm going to do all I can to help send them, after I get to work." In this he was only carrying out the thought which seems to influence nearly all of the students at Tuskegee. A great many of the students and of the teachers have younger brothers or sisters there whom they are helping or looking out for. One young man, a member of the faculty, who has no one of his own family needing help in this way, I happened to learn, is paying all the expenses of a young boy who otherwise would not have been able to remain. I have no doubt there are other similar cases.

What the young man of whom I have just been writing said about the students being obliged to look out for the spare minutes for study recalls to my mind two illustrations which

THESE BOYS WALKED OVER FIVE HUNDRED MILES TO GET TO
TUSKEGEE INSTITUTE.

I had of their methods for doing this. I was walking back to the school from town one day, when I saw coming towards me a lumber wagon drawn by two mules, with a young colored man driving. The day was very hot and the road so sandy that the driver was very properly letting the animals walk. The driver, though, was so intent on something in his lap that I was led to wonder what it was. When he came abreast of me I saw that he had a common-school geography spread out on his knees, and was hard at work learning a lesson. I should not have felt so sure that he was an Institute boy, even then, except that he happened to look up and, recognizing me, brought his hand to his head in the military salute which all of the boys at the school are taught to use.

Another day I had gone down into a field back of the houses in which a number of the teachers live, to watch the operation of grinding sugar cane and boiling down the syrup, which was going on there. One of the faculty who owns a good deal of land raises a field of cane each year and has his stock of syrup made at home. Syrup boiling is an operation which always attracts the children and sometimes older people. There were a dozen small children about, all gloriously happy in various degrees of stickiness. The youngest, not more than a year old, was in charge of a young woman whom I had seen among the students. They were sitting down on a pile of the leaves which had been

stripped from the cane stalks and I had not noticed them particularly, until I heard the girl say, as she propped the baby up comfortably and gave him a fresh piece of cane to suck: " There, now, be a good baby, so that —— can get her lesson." Then she produced a grammar and exercise book and went to work.

James M. Flake, Salem, Alabama : " I came to Tuskegee first in 1894, and stayed between two and three years. I was in day school first, and then, as times got hard, in night school. Then I had to go out to work. I went to Birmingham, and after going about for a while was surprised to find that although I was educated, as I supposed, I could get no work except with day laborers in a foundry. I decided then that a man needed some trade. As soon as I could do so I came back to Tuskegee and began to learn farming. Now, when I get through, I will know how to really do something."

CHAPTER XIII.

THE Bible School at Tuskegee was opened as a distinct department of the Institute in January, 1893. This is not in any sense a theological school. It is so undenominational, or, rather, if the expression may be allowed, so omni-denominational, that among its students may be found not only Methodists, Baptists, Presbyterians and Congregationalists, but Zion Methodists, African Methodists and Colored Methodists, Covenanters, Campbellites, and representatives of various other minor religious sects common in the South. It is not necessary to have a special "call" to the ministry to enter the Bible School at Tuskegee. Women, as well as men, are admitted. Many of those who attend are persons who desire only to do missionary work or to become intelligent teachers of the Bible in the Sunday schools. The need of the struggling little country churches among the Negro population of the South is not so much for preachers of a high grade of mental ability as it is for conscientious, earnest teachers of a wholesome life. Such teachers this department of the Institute aims to train.

Mr. Washington has outlined the purposes of the Bible School in the following words : "What we desire and aim at is to give men and women a thorough knowledge of the English Bible, and

to give them ideas of doing right for right's sake
— to inspire them to go out to work for the
race, to help in uplifting the race and in teaching it right principles."

The Bible School is located in Phelps Hall,
an excellent three-story wooden building erected
expressly for this school by a friend of Tuskegee
in New York.   A bronze tablet in the entrance
hall bears this inscription : —

THIS BUILDING COMMEMORATES A MOTHER'S IN-
TEREST IN THE MORAL AND RELIGIOUS EDUCATION
OF THE COLORED PEOPLE

CAROLINE PHELPS
DAUGHTER OF
ANSON GREENE PHELPS
AND WIFE OF
JAMES STOKES
OF NEW YORK
ERECTED BY HER AFFECTIONATE DAUGHTER
OLIVIA EGLESTON PHELPS STOKES
1892

The building was dedicated in January, 1893,
and among those who were present then and delivered addresses were General Armstrong and
Dr. Lyman Abbot.

The Bible School is in charge of Rev. Edgar
J. Penney, A. M., the chaplain of the Institute,
a graduate of Atlanta University and Andover
Theological Seminary, who is assisted by a corps
of regular instructors and lecturers.   In addition

to lecturers from a distance who come to Tuskegee each year to deliver courses of addresses before the students of this department, the pastors of the three white churches in Tuskegee deliver courses of six lectures each every year. As is the case in the other departments of the Institute, there is, except for a small entrance fee, no charge for tuition, on account of the limited means of the students; and the expenses connected with the administration of the Bible School therefore must be provided for from outside sources. A charge of eight dollars a month secures a furnished room, board, fuel, lights, and washing. The sessions of the Bible School are held only in the forenoon, so that the students can have the afternoons for work, and in this way pay a part or all of their expenses. The students are of all ages. I noticed one woman who must have been more than fifty years old. I learned that she had been for many years at work as a licensed missionary of the Methodist church, but that she had come to the Bible School with a desire to get a more thorough training for her work. She had paid her way while there by doing duty as night watch in the girls' dormitories.

Frequently the students in the Bible School retain their positions as pastors of churches near the Institute while they are at the school. There are four colored churches in Tuskegee, and at times the pastors of all of these have been students. Those who do not have regular employment in this way do missionary work in the surrounding country, some of the men walking out as far as twenty miles each Sunday for this purpose. For several years the students have sustained a regular Sunday service in the county jail at Tuskegee. One Sunday afternoon I was walking in the country near the Institute and came unexpectedly upon one of the country churches just as a service conducted by one of these students was in progress. The church was a weather-beaten little building of unplaned boards, standing in an opening in the oak forest, with no other houses in sight. It stood on posts driven into the ground; the door step was a soap box, the windows had never been fitted with glass, the pews were backless benches, and the pulpit was made by nailing three boards together to form a stand on which a Bible could be laid. It is in such churches as this, and in school houses even less well fitted for their work, that much of the colored population of the South must get its instruction for the present. The need of putting into these buildings the best possible teachers and preachers is all the more necessary.

I have always found it interesting to attend the sessions of the Bible School. Two forenoons each week are devoted to preaching exercises, and two members of the class speak on each of these mornings. These two men have selected their text and subject a week in advance and have prepared an abstract which has satisfied

GRADUATES OF THE BIBLE TRAINING SCHOOL.

the dean of the school. Before they begin to speak they place upon the blackboard an outline of their sermons, and woe be to them if they wander from the line of thought which they have mapped out. There are regularly appointed critics for various details, in addition to general criticisms from the members of the class. I have heard some excellent sermons preached there.

The number of students in the Bible School in a year is usually about seventy-five. A large number of men and women who have come to Tuskegee primarily to attend the Bible School become so favorably impressed with the teachings in the other departments that they remain to enter the academic or industrial classes. Many colored clergymen in the South find it desirable to combine a trade with the profession of preaching, and one of the principles which the Bible School especially endeavors to inculcate is the dignity of such labor, and its value, not only as an aid to the personal support of the preacher himself, but as an example of industry and right living to the people in his community. Among the graduates of the Bible School who are preaching are a tailor, a painter, and several farmers, who learned their trades at the Institute. One undergraduate is a brick mason. One of the graduates of the school is now a presiding elder of his denomination, and graduates from the school have later gone to Morris Brown College, Gammon Theological School, and Yale Divinity School.

The general moral and religious training of the Institute is constant and thorough. There is a regularly appointed chaplain to consider the religious interests of the students. In addition to the chapel services which I have already described, there is a regular preaching service, a Sunday School, a Christian Endeavor Society, a Young Men's Christian Association, a Missionary Society, a Young Woman's Christian Temperance Union, a Humane Society, and various other similar organizations.

CHAPTER XIV.

WITH the close of the school year in May, 1900, the graduates from the three departments of the Institute numbered several hundred. A canvass made by the Institute not long before that date showed that there were also over three thousand students who had taken only a partial course who were doing commendable work. While I was in Alabama in the fall of 1899 I took occasion to visit a number of graduates and students whose homes I could reach conveniently, that I might see for myself what kind of work they were doing, and how they were doing it. A few pages quoted from my note books will give the results of these visits. The men and women whom I saw were not in any way a specially picked lot. A few names were taken from the Institute's catalogue, of graduates reported to be living in the places through which I was to pass, and I selected those which I could reach most easily, obtaining from those upon whom I called the names and addresses of others of whom I had not heard before. Some of those I saw I have spoken of already. I judge that in this way I obtained a fair impression of the general results of the school's work.

The idea of making such a series of visits as this was suggested to me by accident. While in Charleston, West Virginia, with Mr. Washington, I happened to be told that there was a graduate of Tuskegee who was doing excellent work as a teacher of industries at the West Virginia State Agricultural, Mechanical and Normal School, six miles below Charleston. I went down to call on this man, Mr. James M. Canty. What I saw of his work, and what he told me of the work of others of his fellow-students of whom he had kept himself informed, interested me, with the result I have mentioned. I give names and addresses, that any one who may desire to do so may be able to verify my observations.

James M. Canty is a native of Marietta, Georgia. He graduated from Tuskegee in 1890, having been there four years. His story as he told it to me is briefly this : " I had worked some in a blacksmith shop in Marietta as a blacksmith, and wanted to learn the trade more thoroughly. A student whom I knew at Tuskegee sent me a copy of a paper containing an article about the school. As a result I went there. When I reached Tuskegee I had just seven dollars in money, all my worldly possessions. I paid all my expenses by work while I was there, and came out with a balance in my favor. For three years after I graduated I worked at my trade in Marietta. I also worked at my trade during the long summer vacations at Atlanta and at Birmingham. At no time did I have trouble getting work or keeping it, although I was always in shops with white men. I came here six years ago to take charge of the

PERDUE BROTHERS, CONTRACTORS AND BUILDERS.

WILLIAM J. EDWARDS, '93,
PRINCIPAL SNOW HILL
INDUSTRIAL INSTITUTE.

JAMES M. CANTY, '90,
SUPT. OF INDUSTRIES,
W. VA. COLORED INST.

mechanical department and have been here ever since."

Mr. Canty's work as a teacher was very highly commended to me by members of the Board of Regents of the school. I was told that several of his students are already doing good work as blacksmiths and carpenters in the vicinity of Charleston. I saw at the school grounds a water tank holding twenty-two thousand gallons, erected on a steel frame-work seventy-seven feet high. Mr. Canty had built both tank and frame with no help except that of his students, having drawn all the plans himself. He owns a half of a small house in Montgomery, Alabama, which he rents, and when I was at Charleston had just completed a good frame house near the school grounds which he owned clear of any debt and rented for eight dollars a month. It is only fair to this man, and to all of the graduates of whom I write, for me to say that such personal information as this was given me only in response to my questions, and then, in many cases, permission to print it given only because I felt sure it might benefit the Institute if known. Mr. Canty's home is in one of the school buildings. In every way it would compare very favorably with the home of a man in the same position anywhere.

Joseph L. Burks is the proprietor of a grocery at the corner of Fourteenth Street and Third Avenue, Birmingham, Alabama. He was at Tuskegee about five years, leaving there in 1890.

After he left the school he worked in hotels until he had saved $300, and then with this for capital opened the grocery where he now is. He had been in trade three years when I was at his store. His stock then was worth at least $1500, and was paid for. The stock was good and fresh and the store neat and attractive. I happened to encounter this man afterwards in the Penny Savings Bank, the famous Negro bank of Birmingham, just as he was making a deposit. The footing at the bottom of the deposit slip spoke well for his trade.

Robert Mabry is a tailor doing business in Birmingham, on Eighteenth Street, between First and Second Avenues. He graduated from Tuskegee in 1895, after having been there five years. The last two years he was there he took tailoring. He employs one man all of the time and at times another man and a woman. His brother, who is now at Tuskegee learning tailoring, works for him during the summer vacation. His trade is not confined to people of his own race ; he has a number of white men among his regular customers.

George F. Baker, a shoemaker, has a shop at 1129 First Avenue, Birmingham. This man went to Tuskegee in 1894 and stayed five years, graduating from the shoemaking class. When he came to Birmingham, bought some stock, hired a shop and paid a month's rent in advance, he had just fifteen cents left in cash. He had had his shop open four months when I went to see him, and had made a good living. He could tell me just what his business had been for each week. I think he was one of the happiest men I ever saw. He said to me : " I sit here at my work and think of Tuskegee, of the songs we used to sing, and of what it has done for me. I love the place."

David L. Johnson is a druggist at the corner of Avenue A and Twentieth Street, Birmingham. This man's story as he told it to me was this : " As a boy I lived in Dallas, Alabama. A relative who had been to Tuskegee told me of the new school which had been established there for colored people. I entered the day school in 1885, when I was fourteen years old. I worked on the farm. The first vacation I came to Pratt City and went to work in a coal mine. I was at Tuskegee four years, easily making enough in the mines in the vacation to pay my expenses. After I graduated I taught school or worked mining. After awhile I decided to learn pharmacy. To get the money to do this I went to Milldale and went to work mining. I cleared $1500 in a year. I did this by contracting, and working other men under me. I worked driving the heading in the main."

I asked Mr. Johnson why he did not keep on at mining if he could do as well as this, and he said he gave it up because it was breaking him down, physically — which I could understand might be the case, as he is a man of slight physique. What he told me of his work in the mines was confirmed to me by other persons.

The president of the company for which he worked said that he was one of the very best miners the company had ever had. I learned that for some years he had supported his father and mother, and assisted other relatives, and that he is carrying an insurance policy of two thousand dollars on his father's life. I asked him if he had any trouble getting work in the mines on account of his color, and he said : " No, never ; I worked right beside white men a great part of the time, and never knew that I was colored. If a man really wants to work he can find work to do, whether he be white or black. Perhaps it may not be at first just what he would like most to do, but it will be something, and with a chance of promotion."

This man went to Meharry College, at Nashville, and stayed three years, to learn pharmacy. He then came back to Birmingham, and went into business. His drug store was one of the two colored drug stores in the city when I was there.

I asked him how he felt towards Tuskegee. He said : " I love Tuskegee. I mean always to be doing something for the place. I never hear the name spoken even on the street that I do not stop and try to get acquainted with the person who has spoken it, if he be a stranger to me. I do all I can to brace up and encourage the young people who are going there, and to induce others to go. I do not think there is a Tuskegee graduate here whom I do not know." He certainly was able to tell me of a considerable number of students, and where I could find them. In conclusion, he said : " I can sum up my opinion of the methods at Tuskegee in one sentence. It was there I learned how to learn."

Floyd Brooks had just opened a small grocery at the corner of Twenty-sixth Street and Second Avenue, Birmingham, when I was there. He was the youngest of any of the students whom I saw in business for himself, being only twenty years old. He had run an ice business successfully that summer, and planned to peddle coal in the winter. He had worked in grocery stores and hotels after he came from the school, until he got capital enough to start in trade. He said : " I never would have been anything at all if I had n't been to Tuskegee. It taught me how to be economical, and how to do this," pointing to the desk and goods in his little store.

There were seven young women, all graduates of the academic department at Tuskegee, who were teaching in the public schools of Birmingham when I was there. I visited the schools in which all were teaching, and saw them at their work.

Miss Lucile Hunter teaches the fourth grade in the Lane Grammar School. She had fifty-two scholars. That was her second year in the school. She had come directly there from Tuskegee. She had taught the children some of the Tuskegee songs, and they sang them well.

Miss Annie E. Payne graduated from Tuske-

gee in 1894, and had been teaching in the Lane
Grammar School ever since.   She had the junior
second grade when I was there.   She had seventy-five scholars.

Miss Lizzie S. Browning graduated from Tuskegee in 1895.   She had taught country schools
at first, and that was her first year in the city.
She had the first grade juniors of the Lane
Grammar School — ninety-seven in all.   I find
in my note book a memorandum of the pains
she was taking to have the children overcome
the careless habits of pronunciation which they
brought to school with them, such as " lak " for
" like."

Miss Orlean D. Kennedy was in charge of the
sixth grade in the Slater Grammar School.   She
had been there several years.   She had sixty
scholars.   She said : " I feel that I owe everything to Tuskegee."   I found the girls of her
school making a bed-quilt, to be sent to the Alabama State Fair, and she told me that she
taught the girls sewing two days in the week.
I found out afterwards that this was done wholly
of her own accord.   Miss Kennedy showed me,
with a great deal of pride, the " Washington
Library," in the Slater School building, of which
she is the librarian.   This is a library of about
twelve hundred volumes, bought with money
raised in various ways by the colored schools of
the city, and available to any one who pays a subscription of ten cents a month, or one dollar a year.
The library is named for Booker Washington.

The books were selected by Dr. Phillipps, the superintendent of schools in Birmingham, who acted as treasurer of the fund until a sufficient sum was secured.

Mrs. Emma J. Boyd (Miss Parker) graduated from Tuskegee in 1891. This was her second year in the Slater School, where she had the third grade. She had eighty-one scholars.

Miss Rosaline Bradford graduated from Tuskegee in 1893. This was her first year in the Slater School, where she had the fourth grade. She had taught three years in Mr. Edwards's school at Snow Hill, Alabama. Birmingham was her home, and she was educated in the very school in which she was then teaching.

Miss Irene M. Thompson graduated from Tuskegee in 1894. She had the first grade of the Cameron School, with ninety-two scholars. She had taught for some time in the country, but this was her fifth term in her present position.

I interviewed Dr. J. H. Phillipps, the superintendent of schools in Birmingham, in regard to the school work of these young women. He said they were doing excellent work, and then added: " I find in the graduates of Tuskegee who have been teachers in our public schools here a recognition of the industrial factors in the elements of education. They encourage the children to work, and give them much instruction outside of the text-books."

S. P. Foreman is studying pharmacy in the

drug store of Dr. Charles E. Thomas, at 124 West Tenth Street, Anniston, Alabama. He went to Tuskegee in 1889, and remained there five years. It was his plan then to become a druggist, and he gave special attention to chemistry. He had been in his present position two years when I saw him. The drug store of Dr. Thomas is one of the best colored drug stores in the state, and would do credit to any city.

E. J. Williams owns and manages a good "white" barber shop on East Tenth Street, Anniston. He employs three men. He owns his shop and home, and some other real estate. He left Tuskegee six years before, and came to work in the shop where he now is. After a while he became a partner in the business, and then eventually the sole owner. He also owns an interest in a tailor shop, next door to his barber shop.

S. T. Simpson I found working in the tailor shop to which I have just referred. He had not completed his trade at Tuskegee, and was away earning money to go back and finish. I saw some excellent garments of his cutting and making.

George W. Crawford, in charge of the library of Talladega College, Talladega, Alabama, and a student in the college, graduated from Tuskegee and came to Talladega. He hoped eventually to study law. He said: "We all think a heap of Tuskegee."

Two other graduates of Tuskegee who went

A GROUP OF TUSKEGEE SINGERS PHOTOGRAPHED IN THE NORTH.

to Talladega for advanced studies had graduated
from the latter institution just previous to my
being there. Of these, John F. Young had entered the law department of Howard University,
at Washington, and William H. Holloway had
entered the senior class of the Yale Divinity
School.

Miss Jemmie Pierce is in charge of the millinery department of the store of Mr. J. W.
Adams, of Montgomery, Alabama. This is an
excellent store, with a good line of goods, and
requires the services of several persons in the
different departments. Mr. Adams, who is one
of the trustees of Tuskegee, is one of the most
successful business men of his race in the state.
Miss Pierce is a native of Greenville, Alabama.
She was a student at Tuskegee five years, beginning work in the plain-sewing department
and going on through the dressmaking class to
millinery.

Miss Ida Abercrombie is a teacher in ·the
Swayne School in Montgomery. She went to
Tuskegee in 1885, remained four years, and then
after she graduated remained two years more as
a teacher there. I spent one whole session in her
room. She is one of the most capable teachers
of her grade I have ever seen anywhere, and it
was a pleasure to watch her methods. She does
not confine herself to teaching books alone.
There was a good, stout comb on the desk, and
scholars who came with uncombed hair were sent
out to use the comb until they were in a satisfac-

tory condition. Children who came with dirty faces or dirty clothes were sent home with a polite note to their mothers, requesting that they be made tidy before they be allowed to return. The teacher admitted that this policy occasionally caused her to receive calls from very angry mothers, but she said that they generally proved amenable to reason in the end.

Nicholas Abercrombie graduated from Tuskegee and has been employed for eight years as distributing clerk in the Montgomery post-office.

Stephen C. Shepard was a Tuskegee student, but did not remain to graduate. He has been a letter carrier connected with the Montgomery post-office for eight years.

A. C. Perdue is the senior member of the firm of Perdue Brothers, contractors and builders, 315 West Jeff Davis Avenue, Montgomery. Both brothers are Tuskegee graduates, but I saw only the elder. Mr. Perdue went to Tuskegee first in 1888, and graduated in 1891. For three years he worked at his trade, and then returned to Tuskegee as a teacher in the repair shop, that he might have an opportunity to take a course at the Institute in architectural and mechanical drawing. After he had completed that course he returned to Montgomery and went into business with his brother. The firm had plenty of work, the greater part of it from white customers. When I found Mr. Perdue he was on top of a large house on one of the best res-

idence streets of the city, where he was overseeing an extensive job of repairs and alterations.

Dr. Thomas N. Harris is a physician and sur-
geon in Mobile, and one of the partners in a
drug store there. Dr. Harris went to Tuskegee
and remained four years, learning the printer's
trade. After he graduated he returned to Montgomery and taught printing for four years in the
State Normal School for Negroes in that city.
From there he went to Meharry Medical College, from which he graduated, and began the
practice of his profession.

Mrs. I. S. Watkins (Celia E. McDonald) graduated from Tuskegee in 1893. Her husband is
a pharmacist in Montgomery. They own their
home, a pleasant house on South Jackson Street,
at which I called to see her. I mention this
because I wish to speak of her housekeeping —
her work — in the same way in which I have
spoken of the work of the other graduates whom
I visited. At my request Mrs. Watkins very
kindly showed me her whole house. It was
comfortably and tastefully furnished — a good
piano, pictures, books, and all the accessories of
a cultivated home — and was spotlessly neat and
in perfect order. When I said something about
this and spoke of Tuskegee she said, " I learned
order and system at Tuskegee. When I was
there prayers were held in the morning. It was
a rule that the girls must all make their rooms
neat and tidy before they left them in the morning. They were inspected every morning and a

report made. Then if any girl had left her room untidy, Mr. Washington read off her name in chapel, and she had to get up, right there in the eyes of everybody, and march out to go and put it in shape. I hope I was naturally a good housekeeper, but if I had not been I know the dread of the shame of having to be sent out of chapel like that during the years I was at Tuskegee would have made me one."

While I was talking with Mrs. Watkins, her little boy, about two years old and just beginning to talk, came to her bringing a long white roll of paper, saying in his broken words, " I wants to see Mr. Was'in'ton."

His mother unrolled the paper — it proved to be one of the large lithographs of Booker Washington, saved from some window where it had advertised one of his addresses — and spread it out upon her knee, where the boy stood looking at it. " Do you love Mr. Washington ? " his mother asked.

" Yes," said the little fellow, looking from the picture up into her face, and then adding, slowly and emphatically, " I do."

" That's right," she said. " Mother's surely going to send you to be a little Tuskegeean as soon as you are old enough."

The incident interested me as showing the strong impression which Mr. Washington's personality makes upon his students, and it seemed to me full of promise for the future of the school.

A. J. Wilborn, of Tuskegee, graduated from

the school in 1888. For three years he worked at shoemaking in Tuskegee and then opened a grocery store there, in which he has built up a business which is among the most successful in the town. Having decided to erect a substantial brick store in 1900, Mr. Wilborn ordered one hundred thousand brick from the Tuskegee Institute brick yard, at six dollars a thousand, and sent his check to pay for them in advance.

Joseph O. Geddes, who went to Tuskegee in 1895 and remained three years, working in the carpenter and joiner shop and in the paint shop, I found at work in a wood-working shop connected with his father's undertaking business at 1726 Erato Street, New Orleans. This young man and his father both spoke in warm terms of the efficiency of the instruction at the Institute, and of its results as seen in the young man's help in their business.

N. E. Henry, Ramer, Alabama, graduated from Tuskegee in 1893. He taught school for three years at Matthew's Station, in the same state, and then came to Ramer, where I saw him and visited his school. When he went there first there was no school house, and the sessions were held in an old church. Since he has been at Ramer he has built, with the help of the men whose children come to his school, a school house twenty by forty-two feet square, containing two rooms, rudely but neatly furnished. He has at times over a hundred scholars. Before he built an addition to the school house

which gave him a second room, one of the
older scholars, who assisted him in hearing the
lessons, took her class out of doors to hear the
recitations, so as not to interfere with the lessons
going on in the school room. The allowance of
public money for this school had been on an
average only between twenty and thirty dollars
a year, previous to the time I was there. Mr.
Henry rented ground and raised cotton and
corn, with the help of the labor of the pupils, to
earn more money. With what he had obtained
in this way and what the parents of the scholars
had been able to contribute, the school had been
kept open nine months in the year. I asked
this man if he intended to remain where he was,
and he said, " Yes. I think the people need me
here. If I were to go away I am afraid they
would go back to what they were before I came."
This feeling, he said, came from his training at
Tuskegee. When he first went to Tuskegee as
a student he walked from Montgomery, forty
miles, because he had no money with which to
go in any other way. In the three years he was
at Matthew's Station he sent five pupils to Tuskegee, and hoped soon to be able to send one or
more from Ramer. In the spring of 1900 I
saw him at the Tuskegee Negro Conference,
with five of his pupils from Ramer whom he had
brought to get the benefit of the sessions of the
Conference.

A. J. Wood, who graduated from Tuskegee
in 1887, is in business as a general merchant,

A. J. WILBORN, '88,
GROCER.

N. E. HENRY, 93,
TEACHER.

WILLIAM PEARSON, '96,
TINSMITH.

A. J. WOOD, '87,
GENERAL MERCHANT.

at Benton, Alabama. This man taught school after he graduated until he had saved $90 with which as capital he opened the store where he now is. With a desire to learn all that I could about Mr. Wood, and knowing that a man's rivals in business will usually be acquainted with his failings, I went into one of the largest white stores in Benton and asked the proprietor, " What kind of a man is this Wood, the colored merchant down the street here ? "

The merchant, because I was a stranger in town, concluded that I was a drummer, and answered promptly : " You can sell him all the goods you have a mind to· and he will pay for them every time. He's good for all he will buy."

This man has a good store and has built up a good trade. He has the respect of the community. He told me that probably a third of his trade came from white customers, a fact which my own observation while I was in the store would confirm.· While I was in the store and Mr. Wood had been called away to wait on some customers, I stepped to the open back door of the store and stood looking out into a narrow yard behind the building. While I was there the merchant joined me and began to call, " Suke ! Suke ! Suke ! Ho, there, Suke ! "

In response to the summons there began to be a grunting down under the store — like most southern buildings, the store was raised a little way from the ground and had no cellar — and presently there came squeezing out, with considerable difficulty — because he was getting altogether too large to crawl under the sills of the building — an enormous, fat, black hog.

"That is my hog," the merchant explained. "I raise one every year. There isn't any real reason why I should "— he was not married, and boarded out — "but I raise them as object lessons. It doesn't take much of anything to feed them on, except the waste from the store, and you see how fat they grow.

"Then I get the Negro farmers who come in to trade," he continued, "to come and look at my hog, and see what can be done by keeping the animals shut up and fed, instead of letting them run wild and hunt their own feed, as is the custom of most of the farmers here. Then I tell them how they might just as well have their hogs look like mine, instead of being the razor-backs they are. All the farmers need to do is to shut up the pigs in a pen of rails and set the children to gathering acorns with which to feed them.

"I can't start a school here," he concluded; "I tried to, and could not; but if I can't do that I can at least teach the farmers here how to raise hogs as I learned to raise them at Tuskegee."

CHAPTER XV.

THE building up by a Tuskegee student of a school for colored children at Ramer, Alabama, which I have referred to in the preceding chapter, is only one of many similar instances. Just as Tuskegee may be called a child of Hampton, there are springing up, all over the far South, country schools which may be called the children of Tuskegee. The largest and one of the most successful of these is Snow Hill Industrial Institute, at Snow Hill, Alabama, established by William J. Edwards, of the class of '93. The pupils at Snow Hill already number over three hundred every year.

The story of Mr. Edwards's life and the founding of Snow Hill Institute is typical of what scores of Negroes in the South are doing, although in a smaller way, to pass on to others of their race the help which Tuskegee has given to them.

Mr. Edwards was born in a wretched cabin home. His mother died soon after he was born, and his father promptly deserted him. An old grandmother cared for him until he was twelve years old, when she, too, died. A few years later the boy heard of Tuskegee, and, after having walked over a hundred miles to reach the Institute, stayed there until he graduated. He was offered excellent positions at good pay, but refused them all to go back to his old home at Snow Hill, where he opened a school for colored pupils in an old log hut. As this school developed, the excellent effect of its influence in the county attracted the attention of Hon. R. O. Simpson, one of the most prominent white citizens of the county and an ex-slaveholder. This man became so much impressed with the value to the community of the young colored man's school that he gave forty acres of land for a permanent location, and has contributed generously to its support each year.

Snow Hill Institute now employs a force of twelve teachers, all of them graduates of Tuskegee. Instruction is given in academic, moral and religious, and industrial departments. Nine industries are taught, special attention being given to farming. Except for the assistance given him by Mr. Simpson, Mr. Edwards is obliged to depend almost wholly upon his own efforts to secure the money necessary for the support of his school.

Mt. Meigs Colored Industrial Institute was started by Tuskegee graduates in 1885. Miss Cornelia Bowen, one of the first graduates of Tuskegee Institute, is the principal, and the success of the school has been largely a result of her interest and ability. The school now has four buildings, including one devoted to industrial training. There are five teachers and an average of two hundred pupils.

Miss Lizzie E. Wright, '93, has established

WILLIAM J. EDWARDS' FIRST SCHOOL HOUSE AT SNOW HILL.

"WASHINGTON HALL," ONE OF THE PRESENT SCHOOL
BUILDINGS AT SNOW HILL.

one of the most encouraging schools at Denmark, South Carolina, where she has about three hundred pupils. Her experience shows what the earnest efforts of one person can do. She was an orphan, living with an aunt. One day, when she was a girl, a scrap of paper blowing over the ground attracted her attention. It proved to be a part of a circular describing Tuskegee Institute. She could hardly read well enough to comprehend all that the bit of paper said, but with the help of some one else made out enough so that she was fired with a desire to go to Tuskegee. Her uncle told her that if she would work for him the next year in the cotton field he would give her fifteen dollars wages, and that with that she would be able to get to Tuskegee. She toiled through all the hot months, only to have the crop so nearly a failure that the planter could pay her nothing. The next year she began again and did the work all over. That year she was paid and went to Tuskegee, remaining there until she graduated. After graduation she went to South Carolina, and, after looking about for some time for a place where she could begin work, settled in Denmark. After a time, through the help of a white gentleman there, she was able to buy twenty acres of land, with some buildings on it, for $2,000. She has paid all of this but $300, getting the money when and where she could, and while doing it building up her school. She has three teachers besides herself — one of them a young man who graduated from Tuskegee, who oversees the students in the cultivation of the twenty acres of land which the school owns.

John H. Michael, '92, after having occupied the position of Superintendent of Industries at Mt. Meigs Colored Industrial Institute for some time, went to the Slater Industrial and State Normal School, at Winston-Salem, North Carolina, where he occupies the same place. He has made an excellent record as a teacher, especially in the erection of buildings, several large school buildings having been put up wholly or in part by the students, under his supervision.

Abner B. Jackson, '91, has built a good school house at Brackin, Alabama, on the site of an old log hut, in which he began to teach when he went there. He has between two hundred and three hundred pupils, the children coming to school during the summer, and their fathers and mothers during the season of the year when they are not employed on the land.

R. C. Calhoun, '96, has established a school of one hundred students at Eatonville, Florida, where his work has made such a good impression that he has been given one hundred and twenty acres of land for a permanent location. He has a blacksmith shop already, and will add other industries. He intends to plant a part of his land to orange trees. His wife, who was a Tuskegee undergraduate, is his assistant.

Sidney M. Murphey, '87, has taught continuously since graduation as principal of the public school in Eufaula, Alabama. He is now a trustee of Wilberforce University.

In 1899 manual training was introduced into the schools of Columbus, Georgia. Two graduates of Pratt Institute were engaged to take charge of the work in the white schools, and two graduates of Tuskegee to teach it in the colored schools. The work has been remarkably successful. The branches taught are sewing, cooking, and wood working.

It has been impossible for me, in the space at my disposal, even to mention all of the schools which have come into existence as a result of Tuskegee. I have tried merely to give some idea of the work they are doing, and to show over how wide an extent the influence of the Institute already extends.

I have had an excellent opportunity to observe the beginning and development of such schools as these during the years in which I have been goir ; to Tuskegee, since Mrs. Booker Washington has been conducting what she calls missionary work on a plantation about eight miles from the Institute, which has resulted in the establishment of a flourishing school there.

The first year I was at Tuskegee I told Mr. Washington that I wished I might have an opportunity to study the country people in their homes in some place where they were living under typically unfavorable circumstances, in order that I might have a fair chance to see just what material such a school as Tuskegee must plan to deal with. Mr. Washington told me that I could see just such conditions as these without going more than eight or ten miles from the school, and said that he would have me driven out to such a place. A few days later, with Mr. C. W. Greene for a guide and driver, I made the first of these visits. Mr. Greene's long residence at Tuskegee, and his wide experience in all the details of southern country life, have made it possible in the course of these drives for me to get a better insight into Negro life on the plantations than it would have been possible for any one to do under almost any other circumstances.

The plantation which we visited first is nearly eight miles from the Institute. In the course of this drive of about fifteen miles, after we had left the immediate vicinity of the town, we saw only two houses in which white persons lived, except the one on the plantation which was our destination. This plantation comprises fourteen hundred acres of tillage land, nearly one thousand of which are put into cotton each year. At the time of my first visit to this place there were about thirty families of Negroes living there; — the number is somewhat less now. The men, and almost all of the women, worked on the land.

The plantation house was broad and low. It stood at the head of a long avenue bordered by double rows of magnificent water oaks, their foliage as glossy and green in February as if it had been midsummer. Three women were

IDA M. ABERCROMBIE, '89,   CORNELIA BOWEN, '85,
TEACHER.   PRINCIPAL MT. MEIGS INST.

MT. MEIGS COLORED INDUSTRIAL INSTITUTE, ESTABLISHED
BY MISS CORNELIA BOWEN.

washing clothes in the open air, under the trees of the driveway. They were heating the water in iron pots set on stones, between which fires were built. A black sow and her litter of pigs, disturbed from their slumbers in the roadway by our approach, took refuge under a house. The owner of the plantation received us very courteously, and gave us permission to go wherever we wished.

A few single houses for the hands, built near the "big house," were of frame and had one window each, but these were so old and in such poor repair that the roof hardly shed water. The greater number of the families lived far down on the plantation. We drove out to their quarters between hundreds of acres of cotton fields where the strippings of the last year's crop still fluttered on the weather-beaten stalks. We forded three sloughs, in which, as well as in the clay mud of the roads over which we had driven earlier in the day, our carriage and the harnesses on our horses successfully sustained tests which spoke well for the work of the wheelwright shop and the harness shop at the Institute.

We found the people, almost without exception, living in cabins of one-room each, about twelve to sixteen feet square, usually with no window, the lack of which did not matter so much, since both light and air generally were able to pass freely through the cracks in the walls. In each of these one-room houses would be living from six to ten persons, often comprising two families. There was no school nearer than Tuskegee. As a result, there were found to be very few individuals from out the whole thirty families who could read even simple print. There was a little old church between the plantation and Tuskegee, in which there were at times services to which the people might have gone by walking four miles each way.

These were the conditions on this plantation when Mrs. Washington decided to try to do some missionary work there. Her first step was to send and ask permission of the owner of the place. His answer, as I have heard her tell of it, was this : " He just put a colored man on a mule, with a big, fat turkey, and sent him right back to give me the turkey and tell me that I could come down and do anything I wanted to." This encouraging reception was followed by other help later on. After a school was started the use of a cabin was given for it, and land was set aside for the teacher's garden. Both the planter and his wife assisted the undertaking in many ways.

Mrs. Washington's missionary work is apt to be conducted on the principle that cleanliness is not only next to godliness, but in front of it. She selected what seemed to her to be the most promising-looking house in the settlement and asked the woman who lived in it if she could invite some of the people on the plantation to come to her house to a meeting. The permission was readily given. The next Sunday was selected

for the day, and word was to be sent over the
place by a boy. On the appointed day Mrs.
Washington, with two of the teachers from the
Institute, came to the plantation in good season,
bringing with them, along with books and papers which missionaries might be expected to
bring, a good, stiff, new broom. Since Mrs.
Washington had asked to be allowed to use the
house, it was easy for her to suggest that she
be allowed to help make some special preparations. She made the woman a present of the
broom, and then proposed that each sweep a half
of the house, the woman beginning. This was
done, but before Mrs. Washington had nearly
completed her own share, digging the mud
chinking out of corners and dealing thoroughly
with all the dirt, the woman, who had been
watching her, was saying, "Oh, Mis' Washin'-
ton, you jes' lemme take dat broom agin, so Ah
can do mah half ovah." The first lesson had
been learned.

The first meetings were little more than
friendly visits, with some songs and, before the
visitors came away, a prayer. Pictures, music,
and talks with the women and children paved the
way to propose a school. Mrs. Washington tells
of one incident connected with the beginning
of this school : " We carried down some prim-
ers and easy reading books. Quite a number of
men and women and children came to the house
where the week before I had told them the
meeting would be held, and if they did n't seem

particularly interested, were at least pleasant. This was true of all but one young man who stood outside the house all of the time and would n't come in, although he was asked to several times. He seemed to me to look sullen, and I was really afraid of him, and said to myself, ' I don't believe it's any use trying to do anything with him.' But, finally, after I had been around to all the rest and had asked them if they did not want to come to a school, or send their children, I plucked up courage to go and speak to him, because I was determined I would n't let him say he had not been asked.

" So I went out of doors and said to him, ' Would n't you like to come to school ? ' He did n't answer for a minute, and when I looked up to see the reason there were great tears rolling down his cheeks.

" ' Oh, Mis' Washin'ton,' he said, ' Ah 'm so 'shamed, but Ah don' even know mah letters. Ah wants ter learn ter read, evah so much, though, an' if you 'll only jes' lemme take a book Ah 'll go off down in de woods an' learn mah letters there.'

" That taught me," said Mrs. Washington, " never to be downhearted again about the work. What a pity it would have been if I had not spoken to him, for he has learned to read quite well — the last time I was down there he had got up to the third reader, and of course he doesn't have much chance, as he works days on the plantation."

This was the beginning. Before many months it was possible to open a regular school. The owner of the place, as I have said, gave the use of an abandoned cabin ; and a young woman, a graduate of the Institute who had had some experience in teaching, moved in with bed, broom, mop, table, dishes, coffeepot and teakettle, for the little one-room cabin must be not only the school house but also the teacher's home. This teacher, Miss Annie Davis, is a young woman whose education and refinement would entitle her to a welcome in any society. It is hard to fully realize what it must have meant to her to leave home, friends, and all the associations which had made life pleasant, and take up this work. It could not have been for money that she went, for she was to be paid only ten dollars a month, and even this small amount Mrs. Washington had to secure as best she could from such friends as she could interest in the work.

Some of the teachers at the Institute voluntarily became responsible out of their own none too large salaries for the money necessary to provide the teacher with food, but after a few months they were relieved from this tax. The people on the plantation who were receiving the benefit of the newly established school were encouraged to do all they could to help sustain it. They could do this most easily by making contributions of food, fuel, and work ; and such assistance began to be given. One little girl would bring "teacher" two eggs when she came to school; another brought half a chicken; another a "mess of greens." A father would draw a load of wood, and another father would cut the wood into fireplace length. When one of these men went hunting and had good luck, "teacher" quite likely got a 'possum. A record book of all these contributions is kept and the record is read aloud once a month by Mrs. Washington when she happens to be at the school. In the list I have given above I have only quoted verbatim from this record book. For a long time the teacher has been supplied with food in this way.

As is the case at the Institute, the teaching from books at such a school as this is only a part of the instruction. The girls learn to make the teacher's bed, to sweep and wash the floor, to wash dishes, sew and mend. The boys cut wood, sweep the yard clean, raise chickens, and, in a little patch of ground which has been fenced in, cultivate a garden. The children come to school in the day time; their fathers and mothers in the evening. The women learn to read, but they also learn to wash and iron and cook and sew.

When I last visited the plantation the school had been in operation between two and three years. An improvement in the general atmosphere of the place was manifest. A rude but serviceable little church had been built and the attendance of a minister once a month secured.

MRS. BOOKER T. WASHINGTON.

A Sunday school was held each week. I visited the plantation on Sunday. There were over thirty persons at the Sunday school that day. They were neatly dressed, attentive, interested, and thoroughly devoted to their teacher, who certainly may have the reward of knowing that her work is successful and appreciated. She had at that time over fifty scholars, and more would have come if there had been room. Already the fame of the school had spread out into the surrounding country so that scholars from as far as ten miles away were asking to be allowed to come, finding some place to work near or some way in which they could board themselves. Since then Mrs. Washington has bought ten acres of land adjoining this plantation, and had a good double house built on it, into which the school has been moved. Its present accommodations will allow of a broadening of the work, especially along industrial lines.

The true magnitude of the task which is to be accomplished and the conditions which are to be met in beginning such a work as this perhaps may be understood best if I relate one incident which has occurred on this very plantation, an incident not at all unusual in such work.

In the course of the development of the school Mrs. Washington proposed that there be appointed to the position of school committee a man whose general manner and the appearance of whose home had attracted her favorable attention. A woman who perhaps was interested in

a rival candidate came to her and complained
that this man was not a proper man for the
office ; he and his wife had never been married,
she said, although they had lived together for
several years, and had three children.   Un-
fortunately this condition of affairs is possible in
some parts of the South and sometimes may not
excite comment unless for some special reason,
as in this case.   Mrs. Washington went directly
to the man and his wife, and from them learned
that the charge was true.   These people had
been among her strongest helpers, and greatly
interested in having their children go to school.
She said to them, " You must be married at
once ; not only because it is right, and for the
sake of the example on the rest of the people in
the community, but for the sake of your influence
in the school.   The success or failure of the
work here may depend upon it." Ultimately this
proved the strongest argument, and probably the
one which was effectual ; for the father and
mother were honestly devoted to their children's
welfare.   At first, though, they made many ob-
jections ; they had no money for license and
minister, which was probably true.   Mrs. Washington promptly offered to furnish both.   " Come
to my house to-morrow," she said, "and be
married."   They protested that they had no
suitable clothes ; which was quite true again.
She agreed to have clothes ready for both.
They said let them wait until the next Sunday,
and they could come.   She was inflexible.   It

must be the next day morning. Then probably the real hardest reason was brought out — the shame of the public acknowledgment. Here it was that the children and the school triumphed. The parents said they would come.

" I went home," said Mrs. Washington, " in fear and trembling. I hardly dared hope they would come, but I was determined to be ready in case they did." Before nine o'clock the next morning she had procured a license and a minister, and had had a suit of Mr. Washington's clothes made ready to give to the man. She had enlisted the interest of the wives of some of the faculty, and from various sources suitable clothes for the woman were provided. At nine o'clock the man and woman came, eight miles, and were married in Mrs. Washington's parlor ; to which sponge cake and lemonade and a few hastily improvised presents, useful household articles, gave quite a wedding appearance. I am glad to be able to say that I have seen this man and his wife since, in their home, and have shaken hands with them. I think they are honestly trying to make the most possible of their lives for their own sake and the sake of their children. It seems to me a question if many persons will be called on to fight, and if they are so called will win, a harder fight than did this man and woman.

CHAPTER XVI.

I HAVE referred in previous chapters to some of the ways in which the influence of Tuskegee is being extended through the teachings and example of its students; and worthily, too, do they sustain the reputation of their Alma Mater. In addition to the great power for good which is exercised in this way, the Institute has its regularly organized system of what may very properly be regarded as University Extension work. The most important factor in this system is the Negro Conference which assembles at Tuskegee in February of each year. I quote Mr. Washington's own words telling why and how he came to organize this institution : —

"Soon after the Tuskegee Normal and Industrial Institute was established it was impressed upon my mind that much good might be accomplished by some movement which would interest the older people and inspire them to work for their own elevation. I think I first came to think of this when I had occasion to notice repeatedly the unusual amount of common sense displayed by what is termed the ignorant colored man of the South. In my opinion the uneducated black man in the South, especially the one living in the country districts, has more natural sense than the uneducated ignorant class of almost any other race. This led me to the con-

DELEGATES ASSEMBLING FOR THE FARMERS' CONFERENCE.

clusion that any people who could see so clearly
into their own condition and describe their own
condition so vividly as can the common farming
class of colored people in the South, could be led
to do a great deal towards their own elevation.
This caused me to call the first session of what
is now known as the Tuskegee Negro Conference.

At first I sent invitations to about seventy-
five farmers, mechanics, school teachers, and
ministers to come and spend a day at Tuskegee,
talking over their condition and needs. I was
very careful to tell all who were invited to come
that I did not want them to come prepared with
any address or cut-and-dried speech. I very
often find that when the average man is asked
to prepare an address, too much time is spent in
giving attention to rhetoric and too little sense
is put into the address ; so I was very careful to
impress upon all who were invited that we wanted
no formal address, but wanted them to come and
talk about their conditions and needs very much
as they would do around their own firesides.

" To my surprise there came to this first conference four hundred men and women of all
grades and conditions. The bulk of the people
were farmers and mechanics, with a scattering
of teachers and ministers. The morning of the
day was spent in having told in a plain and simple manner what the conditions were along industrial lines. We had each delegate, as far as he
could, tell the number of men in his community
who owned their farms, the number who rented

land, the number who lived in one-room log cabins, and the number who mortgaged their crops. We also had them tell about the educational conditions in their communities. We gave attention to the moral and religious life of the community, and had them tell what kind of a minister they had.

" From the very first we have been surprised at the frankness and directness of these reports. In the afternoon we heard from these same people what, in their opinion, would bring about remedies for the evils which they had described. It was very encouraging to see how clearly the people saw into their own condition, and how often they were able to suggest the needed remedies. If was found that in what is known as the 'Black Belt' of the South at least four-fifths of the Negro people in many counties were living in one-room cabins, on rented land, were mortgaging their crops for food on which to live, and were paying a rate of interest on those mortgages which ranges from fifteen to forty per cent per annum. The schools, in most cases, extended but three months, and were taught, as a rule, in the churches, in· broken down log cabins, or in a brush arbor."

The first conference adopted the following set of resolutions, and each succeeding year a set similar to these has been made a basis for the discussions, such new matters being considered from year to year as may have come up to attract attention.

" 1. The seriousness of our condition lies in
that, in the states where the colored people are
most numerous, at least ninety per cent of them
are in the country ; they are difficult to reach,
and but little is being done for them. Their
industrial, educational, and moral condition is
slowly improving, but among the masses there
is still a great amount of poverty and ignorance,
and much need of moral and religious training.

" 2. We urge all to buy land and to cultivate
it thoroughly ; to raise more food supplies ; to
build houses with more than one room ; to tax
themselves to build better school-houses, and to
extend the school year to at least six months ; to
give more attention to the character of our
leaders, especially ministers and teachers ; to
keep out of debt ; to avoid lawsuits ; to treat our
women better ; and that conferences similar in
aim to this one be held in every community
wherever practicable.

" 3. More can be accomplished by going forward than by complaining. With all our advantages, nowhere is there afforded us such business
opportunities as are afforded in the South. We
would discourage the emigration agent. Self-
respect will bring us many rights now denied us.
Crime among us decreases as property increases."

The second conference was attended by about
eight hundred persons, representing every section
of the South. The attendance has increased
each year. One of the most interesting features
is when the people are given an opportunity to

tell how these conferences have been beneficial to the masses. For instance, at the last session one man said that where in his community before these conferences were begun only two persons owned land, now there are fourteen who do so; few live in one-room cabins and few mortgage their crops; they had not only built a school house but had extended the school year from three to six months. It is a common thing to hear these men report that the community has long since got to a point where no man who is not morally upright can be a teacher or a preacher in it.

The first sessions of the conference were held in the assembly room in Porter Hall, but they soon outgrew the accommodations there. When I first began to attend the conferences the delegates gathered in the rude temporary building which then served for a chapel. Imagine a broad, low building, walled and roofed with unplaned boards, its floor the ground, and the only seats in it made by spiking planks on to posts driven into the earth. From the rafters hang long steamers of Spanish moss, and the walls are trimmed with Union flags looped back with spiked palmetto leaves. Every inch of space in the building is occupied by the delegates and their wives, and late comers who cannot get in cluster around the open windows and doors like bees around the mouth of a hive.

The majority of these men and women were slaves. They see their sons and daughters

A QUARTETTE OF "SISTERS."

CONFERENCE DELEGATES.

learning many things which for their own generation were impossible. They ask, " Is there no
chance for us?" The Negro Conference is
Tuskegee's attempt to answer their appeal.
" O Lord, we want to thank thee for this, our
one day of schooling in the whole year," was the
first sentence of the prayer with which I heard
a grizzled Negro preacher open one year's session.

I turn to my note books again for illustrations :
Father Mitchell, a regular attendant since the
meetings were organized, discoursed on the ex-
travagance of the race. " We's been eatin' too
much terbaccer an snuff," he said. " We's been
puttin' the bridle into our own mouths." At the
same time Father Mitchell is not parsimoni-
ous. It is one of the proudest boasts of this
man that he raises a good fat hog every year to
give toward the support of Tuskegee.

Many of the speakers are hampered by the
lack of words to express all that they would say,
they are so tremendously in earnest. One man
raised an indignant chorus of " You don't done
mean dat," when he said, " The people ought to
practice more intemperance." " Dat's what Miss
Porter (a favorite teacher) said," he persisted,
in response to the cries of expostulation, at
which Miss Porter felt called upon to rise, evi-
dently very much embarrassed, to say, " O Mr.
Harris, I never said that. I said 'temperance.'"
To which the farmer replied, nothing daunted,
" Well, they all knows what I means." This
man's logic was all right, if his diction was shaky,

for when some one asserted that the colored
people had to pay so much money for taxes that
they were impoverished, he retorted, "It aint for
taxes de money goes. What dey pays for taxes
is like dis"—measuring off on a five-foot stick
which he had with him a portion about five
inches long;—"but what dey pays for int'rest is
like dis"—holding up the stick so that its whole
length of five feet was to be seen.

One other man was so diffident about telling
his story that Mr. Washington finally helped
him out by saying: "What Mr. Ligon means is
that after he had made up his mind to get a
start for himself, when he was too poor at first
to own even a mule, he used to go out moon-
shiny nights, when the neighbors would not see
him, and plow with the boy hitched up to draw
the plow." This recital elicited a round of ap-
plause, but when this had quieted down the man
himself was seen to have risen to his feet again,
and he was heard to exclaim, "O Mr. Washin'ton, Ah didn' say dat. Ah never say Ah plow
de boy. Ah say Ah put on de harness an' he
plow me." This distinction being satisfactorily
established Mr. Washington went on to explain
that the important fact which he wanted to bring
out was that the course which this man had
followed had made him the owner of a good farm,
of stock in one of the Tuskegee banks, and of
various other property.

Since the completion of the new chapel the
sessions of the conference have been held in that

building. There is a steady, healthy increase in attendance and interest, which shows that the institution has taken hold on the people in such a way as to give it a permanent influence for good. Although, as would be expected, a majority of the delegates are from Alabama, every one of the southern states usually is represented.

The practical nature of the teaching of these gatherings can be seen from the following list of admonitions printed on a slip of paper which was given to each person entering the church to attend the sessions of the Conference for 1900 :

THINGS TO REMEMBER AND PRACTICE DURING 1900.

1.   Do not be deceived by emigration agents.

2.   See that you treat your wife better than you did last year.

3.   If you have an immoral minister or teacher, get rid of him.

4.   Give the lessons learned in these conferences to your neighbor.

5.   Own a home just as soon as possible. Begin buying one this year.

6.   Keep out of lawsuits. Do not lie around town on Saturdays.

7.   Do not plant too much cotton, but more corn, peas, sugar cane, sweet potatoes, etc. ; raise hogs, cows, chickens, etc.

8.   It is wrong to keep your family in a house with but one room ; have at least two rooms — three are better.

9.   Pay off the old debt as soon as possible, and do not make another.

10.   A three-months school amounts to but little; extend the term to at least six months, by each one taxing himself.

11.   Don't waste money on excursions, whiskey, cheap jewelry, and other things that can be done without.

12.   Do not mortgage your crop; if you have done so, go in other debt as little as possible.

13.   Do not stand still and complain, but go forward — mere fault-finders accomplish little.

Another slip, printed, like the first, in the Institute's printing office, was given at the same time to the women who were present. It read : —

THINGS FOR WOMEN TO REMEMBER AND PRACTICE.

1.   More is gained by going forward than by standing around idling and complaining.

2.   If your minister or teacher is immoral, use your influence against him — this is the right thing.

3.   Do not be satisfied with a one-room cabin — its influence is bad.

4.   Never consent to your husband's going in debt.

5.   Harm very often comes from allowing your home to be a place where young boys and girls congregate on Sundays or Saturday nights — discourage Sunday visiting.

INTERIOR OF TUSKEGEE CHAPEL WITH THE FARMERS' CONFERENCE IN SESSION.

6. Do not spend your money for bright colored ribbons, brass earrings, breastpins and finger rings — never give your children whiskey.

7. Court houses, public auctions, and the like are places where women should never be seen except when absolutely compelled by the law.

8. Visit the school, become acquainted with the teacher, and thus learn for yourself whether he or she is a fit one. Do not encourage your children to tattle about the teacher.

9. Make no demand upon your husband that will interfere with his buying a home.

10. Do not allow any one to be more interested in the education of your children than you yourself are. Make every effort to extend your school term.

11. Do not expect your husband to be mindful of your comforts if you neglect his. It is a part of your duty to see that things are comfortable around the house.

12. Let there be such close confidence between husband and wife that one will not enter into any compact with a third party without the consent of the other.

13. Let every father and mother study the individual character of their children and deal with them accordingly. Make whipping your last resort — never strike children on the head.

14. No one is too old to learn ; do not be content to better your own condition and stop there. Help your neighbors by teaching them what you have learned at these conferences.

The Negro women take just as much interest in the conferences as the men, and frequently are among the most entertaining speakers. One woman, when the conference was discussing the evils of one-room log cabins, got up and said : " I was a widow. I had two children and John had five. I married him and that made seven. He had only one room to his house. I told him he had got to get more, and he got them. I have one room 'specially for cooking, 'cause I don't propose to have everybody see what I cooks. I have learned a heap here at this meeting to-day. Let sardines and snuff and candy and red ribbons alone. Get your man to buy land, just one acre at a time, if he can't get any more than that, and then work it. Some of you men jest want to put us women in the white folks' kitchens to work and feed you, while you walk up and down the road."

The Conference of 1900 adopted the following set of declarations : —

1. More and more, as a race, we feel that we are to work out our destiny through the slow and often trying processes of natural growth rather than by any easy, sudden, or superficial method ; and while we are trying to make ourselves worthy citizens we ask the patience and good will, and appeal to the sense of justice, of our white friends.

2. We desire to reaffirm what we have advised in previous years, that, while not overlooking our rights as citizens, it should still be our main

concern to use our energy in continuing to secure homes, better schools, a higher degree of skill, and Christian character, and in the practice of industry and economy.

3. We believe the race is making slow but sure progress, and we are glad to note the growing interest of the best Southern white people in our elevation, as shown by the various conferences, held by them, for the discussion of the race problem.

4. We would call attention to the fact that our people charged with crime, and in Southern prisons, have, as a rule, little or no education, and are largely without industrial and moral training.

5. We believe that the openings in the South for employment, especially in the direction of skilled labor, were never greater than now.

6. We urge all to become tax-payers and to promptly pay their taxes, to keep out of the courts, to cease loafing on the streets and in public places ; and to prepare to do well the work which the best interests of the community demand.

These declarations should be tacked up in your house that they may be referred to during the year.

CHAPTER XVII.

On the day following what is known as the Negro Conference there is held what is called the Workers' Conference, composed of white and colored teachers in educational institutions for Negroes in the South, and of professional and business men of both races. This supplementary conference was established because many lessons can be learned from the Negro Conference which ought to be discussed and put into practice by teachers in colored schools and by workers in other fields. A considerable number of northern men and women interested in educational work also attend the conference each year for the sake of the valuable information which can be obtained there. The success of the Tuskegee Negro Conference has led to the establishment of similar organizations in other Southern states. The influence for good of such gatherings is very manifest, especially to one who has attended them.

The teachings of the conference are disseminated widely by the hundreds of men and women who attend the sessions, but their voluntary service is not the only agency depended upon to strengthen the influence of the meetings. One member of the Institute's administrative force, Mr. T. J. Jackson, devotes his whole time to advancing the interests of the conference

AN OLD "UNCLE."

FATHER AND SON.

work. In a great many of the towns and counties of Alabama the Negroes have organized local conferences or farmers' clubs, which meet at frequent intervals during the year and make annual reports to the central organization at Tuskegee. In 1900 there were two hundred and fifty of these in existence. Mr. Jackson attends the meetings of these local societies to encourage and advise the members, and organizes many such societies in places where the people have not started them for themselves. His work keeps him in close touch with the farmers. He is able to see to what extent they are putting the teachings of the conference into practice, and in a measure to decide what subjects are most needed to be brought up for discussion at the annual gatherings.

The work which Mr. Jackson does in the state of Alabama other representatives of the school do so far as they can in other states. Quite often some of the teachers, especially the men in the agricultural department, go out for a long distance to hold special meetings of this kind. These meetings, which are thoroughly advertised by means of posters printed in the Institute's printing office, will be held in a country church or school house. Frequently a graduate of the school, or a student who has gone home to work, arranges for such a meeting as this and gets the Institute to send him a speaker to help him in starting what he is quite apt to designate as "a little Tuskegee" of his own. The Negro preachers who have come within the influence of the Institute's teachings are a great help in this work, too, as they go through the country. The farmers and their wives come to the place of meeting prepared for an all day's session. If the meeting is the first which has been held in a locality the plan of the Negro Conference is explained. The fundamental principle which the speakers seek to impress is the value of ownership of land. The people are shown how often they can buy land merely with the money which they waste in foolish expenditure and in the time which they lose in going to town too frequently. As one Negro farmer said, " Too many of us have two Sundays in a week," meaning that they are too apt to spend Saturday loafing around the towns. They are shown what are the most profitable crops for them to raise, and how to raise them. If a man from the agricultural department is going out to hold a series of these meetings, quite often he carries with him his butter moulds and paddles and his cheese hoop. The farmers' wives have been asked beforehand to bring milk and cream with them to the place of meeting. During the day they have a practical object lesson in making butter and in the beginning of making cheese. They are taught the advantage of raising poultry, eggs, and garden truck, and of utilizing the fruits, berries, and nuts with which the forests abound.

I give a few illustrations taken from Mr. Jackson's note books : " One man in Ramer found by practicing the conference methods that he changed from coming out $50 in debt one year to $60 surplus the next. He did this mainly by buying less, and buying what he did find necessary to purchase, for cash. This man had never supposed he could get along without a mortgage." This conference at Ramer was organized by Mr. Henry, the Tuskegee graduate whom I have already spoken of as teaching at Ramer.

"Another man at Ramer tried an experiment. He had always been in the habit of having his wife help him cultivate the land. One year he planted less ground, just what he could take care of himself, and had his wife devote her time to the care of the house and children, to raising poultry, and to such work as that. He kept a careful account of the results of the work of each year, and the second proved so much the more profitable in money as well as in comfort that he ever afterwards followed that plan.

"Another man made a pledge that he would own a piece of land in five years; he had never owned anything before except a mortgage. The first two years he got out of debt and made enough to live on the third year. That year, being free to move, he hired a piece of land, on to which he moved his family. The next year he would make enough to rent a patch outright, and on that he would make enough to buy the land the fifth year."

Frequently land can be bought in large quanti-

ties when it cannot in small, as some one will
have a large plantation which he wishes to dis-
pose of as a whole. In these cases the Negroes
sometimes club together and buy the whole lot,
dividing it up as suits themselves. A regularly
chartered company at Mt. Meigs has bought
about a thousand acres in this way. "A man
by the name of Nickerson, in Russell county,
was so determined to move that he sold his mule
— his whole capital — to pay his debts. He leased
a large plantation for four years, and at the end
of the fourth year made the first payment towards its purchase. He had done this by having his two sons and a brother move on to the
place with him, thus making, as they say there,
'four plows' to work with. He got this idea at
the Tuskegee Conference.

"In one place the women organized a conference because the men of the community did not
seem to be much interested. They signed an
agreement not to wear a mortgaged dress or to
eat mortgaged food, and they lived up to the
agreement. They realized that they could buy
much more cheaply in large quantities and so
pooled their money, each paying a dollar apiece,
at first. With this they bought what they wished
and then divided the goods among themselves."
The women frequently form what they call auxil-
iary conferences, pledging themselves to raise so
many hogs, so many chickens, and so many
dozen of eggs in a year.

"Rufus Herron, of Camp Hill, Alabama, has

A SNAP SHOT ON THE GROUNDS.

ARGUING THE POINT.

become so strong a convert to the conference idea that he offers to pay the expenses of any man in his community, who cannot otherwise afford to come, who will attend the conferences. This man owns a plantation of one hundred and sixty acres." Many colored men now own much larger plantations than this.

Mr. Washington is nothing if not practical. His ability to see a chance to do good is equaled by his promptness to take advantage of the opportunity. An instance of this is to be found in a circular letter which he sent out to the Negro farmers in the fall of 1899, just when the cotton crop was being marketed. The names and addresses of all of the delegates who come to the conferences are recorded, and the names of many other farmers secured. To these men a copy of the following letter was sent : —

To the Colored Farmers of the Black Belt of the South.

"Dear Sir : — We feel that the eight annual sessions of the Tuskegee Negro Conference have done much good throughout the South. The masses generally have made improvement in getting rid of the one-room cabin, in buying land, in using greater economy, in paying themselves out of debt, and in living up to the resolution to better their condition along moral and educational lines.

"But while some progress has been made, there is much yet to be accomplished. The poverty and ignorance of our race demand our most serious consideration. We must work harder this year than ever before to improve the surroundings and elevate the characters of our people. There are over five million Negroes in the South — more than half the race — who cannot yet read and write; and what is worse, ignorance in some localities is increasing faster than intelligence. This alarming fact should lead us to make every possible sacrifice for the education of our children. Instead of spending money for things that we do not need, let us save this money and prolong our school term to six, seven, or eight months. We can do without old, worn-out buggies, cheap jewelry and degrading railroad excursions; but we cannot do without good schools for our children, if we hope to get our rights as citizens. Every community should run its school at least six months, and the way to do this is to begin at once to make preparations for it.

" Last year cotton sold as low as four cents a pound. This year it is selling for as much as seven cents and may go even higher. Now, what permanent advantage will there be to the farmers as a result of this increase? Will they continue to waste and foolishly squander their earnings, as they have been doing for the past twenty years? Now is the time to put in practice the teachings of the Tuskegee Negro Conference. Those who came out ahead last year on four cent cotton ought, at least, to save some money this year on seven and eight cent cotton, and those who have fallen behind while cotton was down can surely pay off those old mortgages now that cotton is up. But if the results of this year's increase in price are thrown away, the next year will find us in no better condition than we have been in the past. It is the duty of all to take advantage of these comparatively high prices, and begin right now to buy homes and farms. Land is cheaper now than it will ever be again. Let each one resolve that he will not let this opportunity pass.

"We still urge that local conferences be organized and maintained in every community. Information and literature may be had by writing to the Tuskegee Institute for them.

"Very truly yours,
"BOOKER T. WASHINGTON."

CHAPTER XVIII.

THERE are many other methods employed to extend the influence of the Institute, in addition to those which I have just described. Some of these are not so far-reaching as others, but no less successful within their immediate sphere. For several years a special effort has been made to reach the home life of the people who live within a radius of about twenty miles of the Institute, through the churches. The direction of this work has been chiefly in the hands of Mr. J. H. Palmer, who, usually accompanied by one or more of the teachers, visits the churches on Sunday. These Sunday talks deal a little more specifically with the moral and religious side of the life of the people than do the conference meetings, but the foundation thought in both is the same — the need of a wholesome physical life as a basis for real moral improvement.

A Farmers' Institute, composed of Negro farmers in Macon county, has been in existence for several years. This was organized by Mr. C. W. Greene, the farm superintendent, and he presides over the meetings, held once a month in the Agricultural Building.

Mrs. Washington's method of establishing schools I have already described. She has sought also to do a special work among the wives of the Negro farmers and laboring men.

Her "Mothers' Meetings," and "Women's Clubs" have a national reputation. She has described how she came to found, at Tuskegee, the first of these : —

"When the women come to town on Saturday with the men to trade, as they often have to do, they frequently have long, weary hours of waiting, while the men spend their time trading or talking. Many times the women have little children that they have to hold in their arms all of the time. I thought it would be a nice thing if we could have some place where these women could come and rest, and where they might perhaps be taught something at the same time.

"I found I could have the use of an old fire-engine house in town for this purpose. It was not a very good place, but it would do to begin in. Now we have some better rooms. I sent a boy around to invite all the women who would like to do so to come there one afternoon. I had n't said anything to anybody about what I was going to do, because I did n't know that any one would come. They did, though, that first day ; and the number soon increased. Very often we have nearly a hundred women at the meetings now, sometimes women who have come ten miles or more to be there.

"We have two rooms now, with simple furniture. We have a cook-stove and some dishes, enough so that we can give talks on cooking and at the same time have the women do the things we are teaching them. In the same way we have one room fitted up as a bed room, and the women have lessons in bed making and how to keep a bed room properly. There are too many of the country homes in which the people do not take the trouble to have any sheets and pillow cases; they just crawl between what apologies for blankets they have, without removing their clothes. I have had a tin bath tub set in the middle of one room, at times, and show them how they can hang a calico curtain from a hoop above it, or curtain off a corner of a room so that those who live in the house, even if it does have only one room, can have an opportunity to bathe. At times we have talks on cutting out and making clothes for themselves and their children, and lessons in sewing. We show them how they can cut pictures from papers, and make little frames for them, and with these brighten up their homes. These are only a few of the many things we do at the Mothers' Meeting. The teachers at the Institute help me a great deal.

"The women are so interested that they do all they can to help. At first I had to get all of the money necessary to pay the rent and furnish what supplies we needed from such friends as I could, but the women now hold a fair each year where we sell things they have made. In this way they have been able to help pay a part of the expenses."

The rooms which the Mothers' Meeting occupies are over the store of Mr. Wilburn, the Tuskegee graduate of whom I have spoken. They are directly on the public square, and hence

CLASS OF GIRLS LEARNING BEE KEEPING.

are easily accessible. They are open all day.
The children have special lessons in cooking,
sewing, and such work.

A library has been established at Tuskegee
city, and a boys' temperance society. The
Humane Society has set up and looks after a
watering trough. Mr. C. W. Greene has gathered together a Sunday school in the city and
superintends the classes every week. Of the
" neighborhood " work I think the most pictur-
esque feature is the care which the students take
of " Aunt Harriet," an old colored woman who
lives alone in a little house in the oak forest.
She is very old and quite alone in the world.
The students not only contribute from their own
small stores of money to her support, but in
other ways have taken almost the whole care of
her for several years. The boys cut wood for
her and make her garden ; the girls wash for her
and bake and sew and scrub.

The students who give their services to make
more comfortable the life of a poor old woman ;
the man who teaches his townsmen to raise
better hogs ; the boy whose example induces his
friend to realize the advantage of a night shirt ;
the city school teacher who adds sewing to her
grade's list of studies ; the young farmer who
goes home and shows his father how to raise two
hundred and sixty-six bushels of sweet potatoes
where only forty bushels grew before ; — all
who do such things as these are doing, even if it
be unconsciously, true extension work.

CHAPTER XIX.

The property of the institution is constantly growing and increasing in value. The Institute now owns two thousand four hundred and eighty-eight acres of land, six hundred head of live stock, including horses, mules, cows, hogs, and sheep; and fifty vehicles — buggies, surreys, wagons, and carts — built by the students in the school's wheelwrighting shop. There are forty-six buildings, large and small, on the grounds.

The total valuation of the plant with its equipment is fully $350,000. In addition $150,000 invested funds from bequests and gifts, and $125,000, the probable proceeds from the sale of the twenty-five thousand acres of land appropriated out of the public domain of Alabama by Congress, constitutes the nucleus of a permanent endowment fund.

Since the work at Tuskegee was begun there have been collected and expended for the founding and support of the Institute $850,000. The annual expense of the school is now not far from $70,000. About $24,000 of this is provided for by the income from the endowment fund, by the annual allowance from the state of Alabama, and by that portion of the income of the Slater Fund which the trustees of that property have allotted to Tuskegee. The students pay for board and other charges, each year, in the neighborhood of $7,500 in cash, besides what they contribute in labor. Even if the demands for admission to the school were not continually increasing, so that the expense of maintaining it is constantly growing larger, there will still be, unless a sufficiently large endowment fund is provided, a need for a considerable sum to be secured each year to meet the balance of the current expenses. Much of this money Mr. Washington is obliged to obtain from generous friends of the Institute in the North, by personal solicitation and by public addresses, frequently having in the latter the assistance of the songs of a quartette of young men from the school.

I do not think that I have ever known a place where a dollar goes farther than it does at Tuskegee. Those who are willing to contribute to help carry on the work of the school may rest assured that they will get the worth of their money. The fear is sometimes expressed that the giving of money to young people for the purpose of helping them to get an education may have a bad effect — may be deadening to effort and ambition. Those who give to Tuskegee may dismiss this fear from their minds. The greater part of the money given to Tuskegee simply furnishes materials with which the students may work, and opportunities to use these materials. The students work, and work hard, to be allowed to stay at the school, and while doing that work, and in doing it, obtain the education which they seek.

It seems to me as if every one who thoroughly examines into the work of Tuskegee Institute, and who stops to consider the history of the Negro race in this country, its present condition, and its prospect for the future, will acknowledge that Tuskegee's mission is one of national importance, and as such deserves the widest possible support.

Ex-President Grover Cleveland expressed this thought very clearly in a letter to Mr. Washington, written in 1899, at the time Mr. Cleveland was rendering very efficient aid towards securing an endowment fund for the Institute : —

" . . . We [the nation] have to deal with eight millions of Negroes, who, though free and invested with all the rights of citizenship, still constitute in the body politic a mass largely affected with ignorance, slothfulness, and a resulting lack of appreciation of the obligations of that citizenship.

" I am so certain that these conditions cannot be neglected, and so convinced that the mission marked out by the Tuskegee Institute presents the best hope of their amelioration, and that every consideration makes immediate action important, whether based on Christian benevolence, a love of country, or selfish material interests, that I am profoundly impressed with the necessity of such prompt aid to your efforts as will best insure their success.

" I cannot believe that your appeal to the good people of our country will be unsuccessful.

Such disinterested devotion as you have exhib-
ited and the results already accomplished by your
unselfish work ought to be sufficient guarantee
of the far reaching and beneficial results that
must follow such a manifestation of Christian
charity and good citizenship as would be appar-
ent in a cordial and effective support of your
endeavor."

Those who wish to make a special disposition
of money which they give to the Institute can
do so. Some prefer to support one or more
individual students. Others would rather establish
or assist some particular industry, or found some
special feature, like the " Parker Home."

The immediate needs of the Institute at the
time I write, in 1900, are $10,000 for a better
equipment of the industrial building, $4,000 for
a hospital building, $15,000 for a library and
administration building, $15,000 for a dormitory
for young men, and contributions to the endowment fund.

Until a permanent endowment fund is established which will assure a steady and sufficient
income to maintain the school, the best results
of the institution cannot be expected. So long
as Mr. Washington is obliged to be away from
Tuskegee for a considerable portion of the year,
occupied in securing money to meet the current
expenses of the Institute, he sacrifices time and
strength which otherwise would be expended
there and in other work in the South for which
he is so remarkably well adapted. He is fortu-

nate in having the assistance of a very capable private secretary, a native of Texas and an experienced newspaper man in that state before he came to Tuskegee, of whom he says : "My private secretary, Mr. Emmett J. Scott, for a number of years has been in the closest and most helpful relations to me in all my work. Without his constant and painstaking care it would be impossible for me to perform even a very small part of the labor that I now do. Mr. Scott understands so thoroughly my motives, plans, and ambitions that he puts himself into my own position as nearly as it is possible for one individual to put himself into the place of another, and in this way makes himself invaluable, not only to me personally but to the institution. Such a man as Mr. Scott I have found exceedingly rare ; only once or twice in a lifetime are such people discovered."

EMMETT J. SCOTT, PRIVATE SECRETARY.

CHAPTER XX.

THE first chapters of this work were devoted to the story of the early years of Mr. Washington's life. It is only fitting that the book should be closed by a further reference to him and to the opinion which people who know Mr. Washington and Tuskegee Normal and Industrial Institute have for him and for his work. My only embarrassment is to know how to select the few examples which I have room to use, from the great number of commendations before me.

In the summer of 1899 Mr. and Mrs. Washington went to Europe, for a few weeks, rest. While there, both in France and in England the constant and kindly social attentions shown them were a proof that the knowledge of their work was not confined to this country. The papers of both countries universally complimented them and their work. The London *Daily Chronicle* said: "Mr. Washington saw long ago that the most important service which could be rendered the blacks was to make useful artisans and workers of them. He founded Tuskegee Institute and has had the satisfaction of seeing this institution grow to its present status of the largest and most important training center of the black race in the world."

The London *Daily News* said: "We have

among us just now perhaps the most distinguished man of color in America. He has come quietly into our midst with characteristic modesty, having no axe to grind on this side, no funds to raise, or anything of that kind. He has come just for a little rest and for the purpose of having a look at one or two things which we are doing, in the hope that he may the better do the work to which his life is devoted. . . . In the work in which Booker T. Washington is now engaged he has, and should ever have, the earnest support of the right thinking people of two continents."

It is often said, and truly, that a man's keenest judges are his neighbors. The Montgomery (Ala.) *Daily Advertiser* is one of the leading papers of the South. Of papers which have a national reputation there is perhaps no other which is published so near Tuskegee and which therefore has so good an opportunity to watch the work of the Institute. The *Advertiser* regularly gives full reports of all the exercises at Tuskegee and has very frequently referred to the school in terms of warm commendation. In 1898, Major W. W. Screws, the editor of the *Advertiser*, after visiting the Institute, published a long article, written by himself and giving a summary of the work done at the Institute, in which he said : " From the day of his arrival at Tuskegee, when he had only modest surroundings, until the present, when his name and that of the institution over which he presides is known over the entire continent, Booker T. Washington has had the absolute confidence of the white people of that community. There is never a word of harsh criticism of him or of his methods. He has been singularly imbued with a desire to cultivate good relations between the two races, and to be of lasting benefit to his own people. He is succeeding in both undertakings. There is nothing of the agitator about him. His ways are those of pleasantness and peace, and as far as his voice and example prevail there will always be the best of feeling between the white and black people of the country.

"It is a blessing for the control of the colored schools to fall into the hands of such a man as Booker T. Washington. It can be said to his credit that colored teachers are found all over Alabama who were educated at his institution, and in every instance the white people commend them for instilling correct notions into their pupils and for impressing upon them the fact that they cannot prosper unless their white neighbors prosper and unless a proper understanding exists between them. It is infinitely better to have teachers who have such notions than to have those who would seek to create prejudice which would inevitably lead to trouble.

"It might be supposed that with so large a collection of colored people, about twelve hundred, in a town of this size, that there would be trouble between the races. There has never been an instance of this kind, and there is not likely to be so long as the influence of President Washington prevails. The white citizens, without exception, say that you would scarcely know of so many colored pupils being here, as they are under the very best of discipline, and good behavior is the rule with all the students. It is really a pleasure to the citizens of Tuskegee to bear testimony to the excellence of the institution and its management."

The Mobile *Register* of June 19, 1899, said : "Booker Washington is right. The solution of the problem lies not in book-learning or in trying to cut the Negro to the measure of the white man, but in teaching him that this is a world where honest labor begets happiness."

The Atlanta *Constitution* for September 25, 1899, said : "Booker Washington was recently given a reception at the place of his birth in West Virginia, at which the governor and other distinguished citizens assisted ; he is shortly to be given a reception at Atlanta. Are these tributes the result of his color or his politics? Not in the remotest degree. They are the result of the confidence and esteem he has won by reason of his high character and his unselfish devotion to the highest and best interests of his race. They are also a recognition of the fact that he has put a remarkable intellectual equipment to uses that may be described as unique. He has chosen to use it in behalf of the elevation and uplifting of his race."

I have already quoted from the words of the

Republican governor and Democratic ex-governor of West Virginia, to which the *Constitution's* article refers. In November of 1899 I heard Mayor Flower of New Orleans, in introducing Mr. Washington to an audience in that city, say: " The motto of Professor Booker T. Washington is to look upward. He is engaged in a noble work. The seeds he is sowing will fall on fertile ground. After he has passed away there will spring up disciples to continue and disseminate his teachings, which will not be circumscribed by environment, nor limited to Tuskegee, which he has made famous, but spreading far and wide will reach all classes of society, whether white or black."

These are testimonies from men and newspapers of the white race. I add to them a few paragraphs from men of Mr. Washington's own race.

Mr. T. Thomas Fortune, the distinguished Afro-American journalist, editor of the New York *Age,* has said of Mr. Washington : " To-day the South possesses no voice stronger than his — that has the nation for an audience when he uses it, that is teaching Christian love and sympathy and national unity with like power and success. The God that lifted him out of bondage has made of him a great power for good in the land. And it is due to the southern people, to all the southern people, to say that they recognize the native ability and the consecration to service — the sustaining of the weak and the lifting up of the fallen — of the man, the tower of strength, who has taken the place so long and worthily filled by Frederick Douglass, as 'the guide, philosopher, and friend' of the ten million Afro-American citizens of the Republic, with whom his lot is more particularly cast ; and to emphasize the fact that one of the strongest elements of his strength and influence is the respect and confidence of the whole southern people which he enjoys in such unstinted measure — a respect and confidence which, added to that of the people of the North and West, have enabled him to erect and sustain a lighthouse of knowledge in the Black Belt of Alabama, whose reflection, whose pervasive influence, is blinding the eyes of ignorance and prejudice, so that men may see the beauty and the wealth that abound in Nature, and thus intelligently lay hold upon them for their use and comfort, and that they may see and imbibe that reverence for the Creator and love of mankind in which the happiness of the people and the strength of the nation abide."

Mr. R. W. Thompson, of the *Colored American,* has said : " The most remarkable Afro-American of this generation is Booker T. Washington. As was said of Frederick Douglass, he is not only a great Negro — he is a great man. . . . Mr. Washington stands for a definite idea. He is the pioneer apostle of industrial training for the Negro, as the fundamental principle in the solution of the vexatious race problem. . . . Mr. Washington's work is not finished, but the prin-

ciples of industrialism are so firmly imbedded in
the intelligence and affection of the nation that
prejudice and criticism are without power to
injure. Tuskegee long ago passed the experi-
mental stage. It is an enduring monument to
the industry, sagacity, and high moral purpose of
its eminent founder."

TO BOOKER T. WASHINGTON.

Beside our way the streams are dried,
And famine mates us side by side.
Discouraged and reproachful eyes
Seek once again the frowning skies.
Yet shall there come, 'spite storm and shock,
A Moses who shall smite the rock,
Call manna from the Giver's hand,
And lead us to the promised land.

PAUL LAURENCE DUNBAR,
in *Tuskegee Student.*

In the fall of 1899 Mr. Washington published
a book entitled "The Future of the American
Negro," which immediately attracted universal
attention as one of the most important contributions to the literature of the race question. From
the great number of reviews of the book I make
a few quotations to show the very general interest taken in it.

Charles W. Chesnutt, in *Saturday Evening
Post:* "Mr. Washington may be considered, in
relation to education, as the prophet of the
practical. While he is hopeful of his race, and

believes in the ultimate triumph of the forces of progress, which in the end make for justice, the future of the Negro which he discusses is that of to-morrow, as growing out of the conditions of yesterday and to-day; and as he believes in getting the foundations of an argument, as well as of an education, properly laid, he gives to the present a large part of his attention."

Sunday School Times: "No man of the colored race commands more than Booker T. Washington the attention of the American people. His moderation in judgment, his far-sightedness, and his lively appreciation of the difficulties which beset social problems, have earned him this confidence."

The Outlook: "No man in the present decade has thrown so much light on the difficult problem presented by the race conditions in the South as Mr. Booker T. Washington. He has done this by his deeds even more than by his words. He has commended himself to the best elements in his own race and in the white race, both South and North. He has had amazing success in overcoming both race and sectional prejudice, and he has done this, not by palterings or evasions, not by using words in a double sense, not by giving one message to the colored people, another to the Southern whites, and a third to the Northern whites, not by yielding to prejudice, sectional or racial, not by presenting as a compromise a mosaic-work platform made up of incongruous principles, but by his clear perception and cour-

SLATER-ARMSTRONG MEMORIAL TRADES' BUILDING.

ageous but always non-polemical presentation of fundamental principles."

The Chicago Inter-Ocean: "When Booker T. Washington writes or speaks, all nationalities and people can well afford to read or listen. He is easily the foremost and ablest man of color living. He is a brainy, scholarly man, practical in all his methods. He is a natural organizer, who, amid such discouragements as would have enervated most men, has persevered until he has built up an institution which has been a blessing to his race ; and more, by his public addresses he has molded a public sentiment wide-reaching in its good effect."

Rocky Mountain News (Denver) : " Booker T. Washington is recognized as probably the foremost colored writer on social and industrial topics."

The Independent (New York) : "The practical wisdom of Mr. Washington, as illustrated in this book, deserves all praise, and by his race he is generally accepted as their most distinguished leader. The work that he has done at Tuskegee is simply marvelous. He has built up an institution which is a town, and he has an immense task before him in giving it an endowment. But he is young and vigorous and full of faith, and we believe he will do it."

Chicago Evening Post: " Booker Washington is to-day the most widely known and most influential representative of his race. He has eminently the ear of the public. And he has earned this right by what he has done as well as by what he has said. The Normal and Industrial Training School which he has built up at Tuskegee, Ala., is well known all over the country. Educated himself at General Armstrong's Hampton Institute, he has gone down into the heart of the Black Belt and put into force all the most characteristic lessons which he had learned there."

Houston Post (Texas): "Booker T. Washington is the acknowledged spokesman of the Negro race in the South. Besides possessing the well-rounded equipment which leadership requires, he occupies the position of president of the Normal and Industrial School at Tuskegee, Ala., where he is engaged in teaching the young scions of the Negro race how they may earn competent livelihoods and at the same time contribute to the material upbuilding of the South."

Florida Times-Union and Citizen: "The political Negro will not accept Booker Washington as a prophet, but he is doing more for the race than all its bishops, and the next generation will arise and call him blessed. The whites of the South long since recognized in him a prominent factor in its industrial and political development, and hailed him as a statesman as well as the leader well worthy of a following of ten millions."

San Francisco Argonaut: "While the race problem of the South is the most important with which Americans of this generation have to deal, it is an encouraging sign that from among the Negroes themselves should arise such a man as

Booker T. Washington, at once a counselor and a model."

Chicago Times-Herald: "Those who know Mr. Washington's work in uplifting his people recognize that in him the colored race of this country has its Moses; that he has come nearer to solving the Negro problem than anyone that has yet attempted its solution, and that the way he points out for his brethren is the way he has traveled himself and found successful. What he tells his race is that their salvation lies in making themselves industrially capable, that the world wants their labor, their energy, and the fruits of their toil."

The Interior: "The best mind developed by the Negro race in America thus far is Booker T. Washington. He saw through the fog of the Negro problem years ago. He saw that radical and thorough-going reform was necessary in the education of the Negro, and in his ideas. He has done, and is doing, more for the white men of the South, and for the general prosperity of the South, than has been done by all the statesmen and politicians put together. This is fully appreciated by the intelligent white people of the South."

Rev. George B. Eager, in *Woman's Work* (Montgomery, Ala.) : "The South, no less than the North, has reason to be grateful that the well known principal of the Tuskegee Institute has been induced to put into definite and permanent form the ideas regarding the Negro and his future to which he had already given more or less publicity though the platform, the magazines, and the newspapers. The appearance of this book, and the general acceptance of the leading ideas it stands for, will mark an epoch in the history of the South, and, if I mistake not, make a priceless contribution toward the solution of the race problem. The author is well known to our people. He has earned the right to speak to whites and blacks on this subject."

Review of Reviews: " Mr. Washington has written a book that will undoubtedly be very widely read by the northern friends of the work of Tuskegee, and, what is perhaps more to the purpose, it will be read by intelligent Southerners who believe that Tuskegee holds the key to the ultimate solution of the race problem in their section."

New York Commercial Advertiser: " It would hardly be too much to say that the assurance of a worthy future for the Negro race in this country is its capability to produce a man like the author of this book. Among all that has been written on this vexed topic Mr. Washington's review and forecast of his race seems to be the truest and most comprehensive.

" If it be asked what distinguishes Mr. Washington's point of view from other writers on this topic, the answer, it would seem, must be that he emphasizes the creation of industrial values in the Negro, and strives, first, to develop his moral and intellectual manhood as an industrial unit.

He is a pronounced individualist, a preacher of the gospel of self-help for the Negro."

If I were to add my own tribute to those which I have given — and the high esteem which Mr. Washington's life has caused me to have for him during the years I have been associated with him makes me wish to do so — it would be this : Not only has he so taught the students of Tuskegee as to cause them to become industrious, law-abiding, respected, and self-respecting men and women, but he has had the power to inspire in their hearts a desire to do something to help others — a desire to pass on to others the help which Tuskegee has given to them. This seems to me to be the dominant note of the whole institution.

Mr. Washington has said of himself when at Hampton : " I resolved when I had finished the course of training that I would go into the far South, into the Black Belt of the South, and give my life to provide the same kind of opportunity for self reliance and self-awakening that I had found provided for me at Hampton." He has been able to impress this ambition upon those who have been his pupils. The feeling of the students almost universally seems to me to be that the help which generous friends have afforded to Tuskegee Institute is a trust for which its representatives are responsible ; it is their duty and their privilege to fulfill that trust by helping others to become what the Institute has helped them to be. They realize that the real Tuskegee is not merely a school in a county town in Alabama, but an influence for good throughout the whole South, to be spread wider and stronger each year by their consistently putting into practice the principles which the Institute has taught them.

APPENDIX

Appendix

FACULTY

The faculty and the various executive departments of Tuskegee Normal and Industrial Institute were composed as follows for the school year 1899–1900:

STATE COMMISSIONERS.

GEORGE W. CAMPBELL,	Tuskegee, Ala.
LEWIS ADAMS,	Tuskegee, Ala.
CHARLES W. HARE,	Tuskegee, Ala.

BOARD OF TRUSTEES.

GEORGE W. CAMPBELL, President,	Tuskegee, Ala.
REV. GEORGE L. CHENEY, Vice-President,	Leominster, Mass.
REV. R. C. BEDFORD, Secretary,	Beloit, Wis.
WARREN LOGAN, Treasurer,	Tuskegee, Ala.
LEWIS ADAMS,	Tuskegee, Ala.
CHARLES W. HARE,	Tuskegee, Ala.
BOOKER T. WASHINGTON,	Tuskegee, Ala.
J. W. ADAMS,	Montgomery, Ala.
JOHN C. GRANT, LL.D.	Chicago, Ill.
REV. GEORGE A. GORDON,	Boston, Mass.
REV. CHARLES F. DOLE,	Boston, Mass.
J. G. PHELPS-STOKES,	New York, N. Y.
S. C. DIZER,	Boston, Mass.
WM. H. BALDWIN, Jr.	New York, N. Y.
R. O. SIMPSON,	Furman, Ala.

COMMITTEE ON INVESTMENT OF ENDOWMENT FUND.

WM. H. BALDWIN, JR.   J. G. PHELPS STOKES.

EXECUTIVE COUNCIL.

BOOKER T. WASHINGTON,	Principal.
WARREN LOGAN,	Treasurer.
JOHN H. WASHINGTON,	Director of Mechanical Industries.
M. T. DRIVER,	Business Agent.
G. W. CARVER, Director of Agricultural Department.	
EDGAR J. PENNEY,	Chaplain.
JAMES D. MCCALL,	Director of Academic Department.
JULIUS B. RAMSEY,	Commandant.
JAMES N. CALLOWAY,	Manager Marshall Farm.
MRS. JOSEPHINE B. BRUCE,	Lady Principal.
MRS. BOOKER T. WASHINGTON,	Directress of Mechanical Industries for Girls.

ACADEMIC DEPARTMENT.

JAMES D. MCCALL, Director,	Chemistry.
BOOKER T. WASHINGTON,	Mental and Moral Philosophy.
WARREN LOGAN,	Bookkeeping.
BUTLER H. PETERSON,	Mental and Moral Philosophy; Mathematics.
J. R. E. LEE,	Mathematics.
FREDERICK C. JOHNSON,	Mathematics.
JOHN J. WHEELER,	Mathematics; Chemistry.
J. W. MYERS,	Physics.
EDGAR WEBBER,	Civics.

CHARLES WINTER WOOD, Grammar; Elocution.
ALONZO H. KENNIEBREW, M. D. Physiology.
MRS. IDA T. McCALL, History.
ROSA MASON, Reading; Grade Work.
SUSAN D. COOPER, Geography.
ELIZABETH W. MORSE, Writing; [1] Vocal Music.
SUSAN H. PORTER, Pedagogy; Grade Work.
MRS. A. U. CRAIG, Grade Work.
DANELLA E. FOOTE, Assistant to the Director.
MABEL L. KEITH, Grammar.
MRS. SARA P. GREENE, Reading; Grade Work.
MRS. A. H. KENNIEBREW, Grammar.
AZALIA THOMAS, Gymnastics.
SARAH L. HUNT, Grade Work.
CARRIE L. SPIES, Grade Work.
EDNA A. SPEARS, Grade Work.
LYDIA C. ROBINSON, Grade Work.
CLARA B. COY, Grade Work.
IDA A. MORGAN, In Charge of Grades; Writing.
DAYSE D. WALKER, Reading; Grade Work.
ARSINE E. JONES, Training School.
LULA M. CROPPER, Critic in Charge Training School.

LIZZIE BAYTOP, Librarian.
COLUMBUS A. BARROWS, Night School, Marshall Farm.

AARON COAR, Night School, Marshall Farm.
EMMA T. NESBITT, [1] Clerk.

MUSICAL DEPARTMENT.

CHARLES G. HARRIS, Vocal Music; Leader of Choir.
ELIZABETH W. MORSE, [1] Instrumental Music; Writing.
SHERMAN W. GRISHAM, Band Master; Leader of Orchestra.

[1] Part of year

·NURSE TRAINING DEPARTMENT.

A. H. KENNIEBREW, M. D.,   Physician in Charge.
S. M. SMITH,   Head Nurse.

PHELPS HALL BIBLE SCHOOL.

REV. EDGAR J. PENNEY, Dean; Introduction to the Bible; the Life of Christ; Pastoral Theology.
REV. BUTLER H. PETERSON, Bible History; Sacred Geography.
MICHAEL B. STEVENS,   Sociology; Gymnastics.
MRS. A. U. CRAIG,   English.

INDUSTRIAL DEPARTMENT.

JOHN H. WASHINGTON,   Director.
MRS. BOOKER T. WASHINGTON, Directress of Domestic Industries for Girls.
JOHN H. PALMER,   Assistant to Director.
LEWIS ADAMS,   Tinning.
R. B. WILLIAMS,   Wheelwrighting.
JOHN W. CARTER,   Carpentry.
GEORGE B. EVANS,   Carpentry.
M. B. GARNER,   Carpentry.
SOLOMON C. CONYERS,   Blacksmithing.
AUGUSTUS RAYFIELD, Architectural and Mechanical Drawing.
BERNARD NESBITT,   Assistant in Drawing.
ARTHUR U. CRAIG,   Electrical Engineering.
JAMES M. GREENE, Plastering and Brick Masonry.
JOHN C. GREEN, House and Carriage Painting.
WILLIAM A. RICHARDSON,   Assistant in Painting.
WILLIAM GREGORY,   Brick Making.
HARRY E. THOMAS, Founding, Plumbing, and Machine Work.

HENRY E. COOPER, Harness Making and Carriage Trimming.
WILLIAM M. ALLEN, Shoemaking.
J. W. GAINES, Tailoring.
D. R. FARMER, Assistant in Tailoring.
MRS. W. J. CLAYTOR, Assistant in Tailoring.
CHARLES ALEXANDER, Printing and Binding.
LAVINIA E. DEVAUGHN, Dressmaking.
BESSIE PHONE, Assistant in Dressmaking.
ELIZA S. ADAMS, Plain Sewing and Millinery.
LAURA E. MABRY, Laundering.
LILLIE HODGES, Assistant in Laundering.
ROSE MILLER, Mattress Factory.
EMMA T. NESBITT, [1] Cooking.
ALICE PINYON, Cooking.
MRS. A. K. HAMILTON, In Charge of Sales Room.

AGRICULTURAL DEPARTMENT.

GEORGE W. CARVER, Director; Instructor in Scientific Agriculture; Dairy Science.
CHARLES W. GREENE, Practical Agriculture; Farm Manager.
WILLIAM V. CHAMBLISS, In Charge of Dairy Herd.
WILLIAM J. CLAYTOR, Stock Raising.
CRAWFORD D. MENIFEE, Horticulture; In Care of Grounds.
C. A. WARREN, Horticulture.
G. W. OWENS, Assistant in Scientific Agriculture.

BOARDING DEPARTMENT.

M. T. DRIVER, Business Agent.
JOHN H. PALMER, Assistant.
JULIUS B. RAMSEY, Boys' Department; Military Science.

[1] Part of year.

H. W. SEALS,
MRS. J. B. BRUCE,   Principal Girls' Department.
MRS. FRANCES B. THORNTON,   Assistant to Lady
    Principal, and Matron.
HENRY G. MABERRY,   Commissariat.
HORACE S. SCURRY,   Steward, Teachers' Home.
CHARLES L. DIGGS,   Custodian of Buildings.

ADMINISTRATION.

EMMETT J. SCOTT,   Private Secretary to Principal.
ROBERT W. TAYLOR,   Northern Financial Agent.
CHARLES H. GIBSON,   Head Bookkeeper.
LEONARD C. FOSTER,   Assistant Bookkeeper.
THOMAS J. JACKSON,   Negro Conference Agent.
MOSES B. LACY,   Cashier.
NATHAN HUNT,   Stenographer.
SUSIE B. THOMAS,   Stenographer.
EDWARD H. WESTON,   Stenographer.
LAVISA M. CRUM,   Stenographer.
FRANK E. WINTER,   Stenographer.
JAMES B. WASHINGTON,   Clerk ; Postmaster.
C. A. GILMORE,   Registration Clerk.

LECTURERS.

REV. C. O. BOOTHE, D.D.
T. THOMAS FORTUNE.
REV. FRANCIS J. GRIMKE, D.D.
RT. REV. W. J. GAINES.
RT. REV. GEORGE W. CLINTON, D.D.

PRESENT LOCATION AND EMPLOYMENT OF THE CLASS OF 1899.

COLTON ANDREWS, 138 No. Butler St., Atlanta, Ga.
Brickmaker.

MARTIN L. BARNES, 350 Dearborn St., Mobile, Ala.
Working at his trade of brickmasonry.

MATTIE I. BENSON, Kowaliga, Ala.
Teacher of sewing in Kowaliga Industrial
Institute,

CHARLES S. BOWMAN, Quindaro, Kan.
Superintendent of industries, Industrial
School.

FREDERICK A. BOYD, Jackson, Tenn.
Working at his trade of brickmasonry.

NETTIE L. BUCHANAN, Troy, Ala.
Teacher in Troy Industrial School.

WALTER S. BUCHANAN, Aiken, S. C.
Teacher in Schofield Industrial Academy.

JOHN EVANS BUTLER, Tuskegee, Ala.
Taking post-graduate course in wheelwrighting.

EDWARD N. BROADNAX, Tuskegee, Ala.
Painter.

ANNIE L. CAMPBELL, Nixburg, Ala.
Acting principal of Cottage Grove Academy.

ALLIE L. DUVALL, Dawson, Ga.
Assistant teacher in Dawson public school.

G. A. FALLINGS, New Lewisville, Ark.
Not heard from.

F. E. FEISER, 567 Adams St., Vicksburg, Miss.
Teacher in the county schools.

LEONARD C. FOSTER, Tuskegee, Ala.
Assistant bookkeeper at the Institute.

GEORGE A. GOODRUM, Nixburg, Ala.
Teacher in Cottage Grove Academy.

BEATRICE M. GRAINE, 152 Elm St., Paw Paw, Mich.
Teacher in county school.

WILLIAM A. GRAY,   Cambria, Va.
In charge of farm at the Christianburg Industrial Institute at Cambria.

MANCESSOR HAIR,   Newberry, S. C.
Working at his trade of brickmasonry.

SHEPHERD L. HARRIS,   Maysville, S. C.
Instructor in Carpentry.

GEORGE W. HENDERSON,   Montgomery, Ala.
Baker.

ANNIE HENDERSON,   Tuskegee, Ala.
Assistant matron in students' dining room
at the Institute.

LILY M. HODGES,   Tuskegee, Ala.
Assistant instructress in laundry.

PINKSTON HOWARD,   Tuskegee, Ala.
Student in Phelps Hall Bible School.

EDGAR D. HOWARD, 362 Hudson St., New York, N. Y.
Working in drug store preparatory to taking a course in pharmacy.

WARREN W. JEFFERSON,   Montserrat, British West
Principal of Industrial School,   Indies.

JOSEPH LEVETTE,   Tuskegee, Ala.
Journeyman brickmason.

J. G. LOWE,   Waugh, Ala.
Teacher in Mt. Meigs Industrial Institute.

JAMES B. NESBITT,   Tuskegee, Ala.
Assistant instructor in architectural and
mechanical drawing at the Institute.

EGELINA C. O'NEAL,   Columbus, Ga.
In charge of industries for girls in Columbus public schools.

FLORINE PATTERSON,   Tuskegee, Ala.
Teacher in county school.

MARY ELLA PERRY, Tuskegee, Ala.
Taking a post-graduate course in dressmaking.
JOHN H. PINKARD, Jenefer, Ala.
Teacher in public schools of Calhoun county.
ELIZABETH E. PLUMMER, 215 No. Rues St.,
Teacher. Pensacola, Fla.
MINNIE L. RHODES, Greensboro, Ala.
Teacher in public schools.
WILLIAM J. SHOALS, Clear Creek, Indian Territory.
ALICE R. SIMMS, 34 W. Grand Ave., Des
Sewing and housekeeping. Moines, Iowa.
R. C. M. SIMMONS, Concord, N. C.
Newspaper work.
BRYANT SIMPSON, West Point, Ga.
Tailor.
ANNIE L. SMITH, Tuskegee, Ala.
Clerk in store.
ANNIE L. TAYLOR, Montgomery, Ala.
Teacher in public schools.
MATTIE E. VAN HORNE, Tuscaloosa, Ala.
WILLIAM W. WILSON, Pensacola, Fla.
Principal Escambia High School.
R. E. WILLIAMS, Newberry, S. C.
SARAH J. WILLIAMS, Snow Hill, Ala.
Instructress in sewing at Snow Hill Institute.

PHELPS HALL BIBLE SCHOOL GRADU-
ATES, 1899.

WILLIAM C. CHEERS, Tuskegee, Ala.
Student in academic department.
GEORGE GRINTER, Tuscaloosa, Ala.
Student Stillman Seminary.
ADA M. HANNON, Forest Home, Ala.
Teacher.